A Decade of Mozambique

A Decade of Mozambique

Politics, Economy and Society
2004–2013

By

Joseph Hanlon

TUTA SUB AEGIDE PALLAS · 1683 ·

BRILL

LEIDEN | BOSTON

The chapters in this book were previously published in Brill's *Africa Yearbook. Politics, Economy and Society South of the Sahara* 2004–2013.

This publication has been typeset in the multilingual 'Brill' typeface. With over 5,100 characters covering Latin, IPA, Greek, and Cyrillic, this typeface is especially suitable for use in the humanities.
For more information, please see www.brill.com/brill-typeface.

ISBN 978-90-04-30112-2

This book is printed on acid-free paper.

Contents

Mozambique in 2004

The election of a new president dominated Mozambican politics. Frelimo's ('Frente de Libertação de Moçambique') Armando Guebuza won a flawed but convincing victory, suggesting that Mozambique is to be an elected one party state on the model of Botswana and South Africa. Guebuza takes over as president from Joaquim Chissano, whose attempt to stand again as candidate for election was blocked by Frelimo. GDP growth continues at more than 8% per year and there was considerable further expansion of the mineral and energy sector, but more than half the population live in extreme poverty and unemployment is rising. Growth seems to benefit only those who are already better off.

Domestic Politics

The *presidential and parliamentary elections* on 1–2 December gave an overwhelming victory to Frelimo, which has governed Mozambique since independence in 1975. This was the third national multiparty election since the end of the war of destabilisation in 1992. Although support for Frelimo has been declining slowly, in the 2004 election support for the opposition collapsed completely, with Renamo ('Resistência nacional Moçambicana') president Afonso Dhlakama losing more than one million votes. Turnout was 3.3 m (about 43% of registered voters) compared to 5.3 m in 1999 and 1994. Frelimo won 160 seats in parliament compared to only 90 for Renamo. Nearly all observers, including Frelimo, predicted a close race similar to 1999, and the low turnout and *collapse of the opposition* came as a complete surprise. Equally unexpected was the poor showing of the first serious third

 | DOI 10.1163/9789004301122_002

party, 'Partido da Paz, Democracia e Desenvolvimento' (Party of Peace, Democracy and Development/PDD) and its leader Raul Domingos. He and Guebuza had been the two lead negotiators in the 1990–92 Rome peace talks, but Domingos was expelled from Renamo in 2000. He ran a well-funded and properly organised campaign but gained less than 3% of the vote and PDD only 2%, which was not enough for a parliamentary seat (which requires at least 5% of the national vote).

Frelimo's declining vote is linked to *public discontent* with widespread corruption and what is widely described as the 'deixa andar' ('don't bother, let it go') attitude of the Chissano government: both are contrasted with the integrity, lack of corruption and activism of the Samora Machel era. Grassroots resentment at the rise of corruption and a new self-serving elite was widely reported by Frelimo organisers to be behind the close election in 1999. Under the constitution, Chissano could have stood for one more term, but his bid was rejected at the 2002 Frelimo party congress. Guebuza was chosen instead, with the backing of the Frelimo old guard. This is not a generation change, since both had senior positions in the 1964–74 liberation war and Guebuza, at 62, is only three years younger than Chissano. But Guebuza is an activist on the Samora model, and he spent the year after the congress travelling extensively throughout the country, rebuilding the party base to ensure its loyalty and to ensure that it encouraged the loyalists to vote, which did occur.

Over the past 35 years, *Frelimo* has put party unity above all other goals: there have been no splits and, in recent years, no expulsions. Chissano remains on the 15-member political commission and campaigned for Guebuza. Frelimo has been careful to bring into the party and into government posts political figures who might be considered threats. For example, Luisa Diogo was clearly a rising star, and only joined the party in the late 1990s when she was already deputy finance minister. She became finance minister in 2000 and was named prime minister on 17 February, to replace Pascoal Mocumbi (who moved to the Netherlands to head the European-Developing Countries Clinical Trial Partnership).

Renamo, originally created by Rhodesian security services and promoted by the South African apartheid military, gained a local base of sorts during the 1976–92 destabilisation war. As part of the peace accord, and with substantial help from donors, it became the main opposition political party. But guerrilla leader Afonso Dhlakama kept extremely tight personal control and failed to build an effective party, and good organisers who were seen as a threat, such as Raul Domingos, were expelled. Furthermore, he ran a very negative campaign, stressing his claim that the 1994 and 1999 elections had been stolen from him by fraud, and ignored advice from sister parties such as the British Conservative Party to mount a more positive campaign stressing what he would do as president. The result was that many who voted for the opposition in the past saw no point in voting, since Dhlakama himself was saying it was pointless. Dhlakama was also hurt by a lack of money. Influential backers, such as the US, had decided that he had no chance of creating a real party that could win an election, and funding dried up.

Discontented electors did not opt for any of the 19 other parties on the ballot paper, none of which won parliamentary seats. The low vote for Raul Domingos, a known figure with a well-financed campaign, surprised most observers. One factor in the *low turnout and low support for the opposition* was that none of the parties presented serious alternative policies – and there is, indeed, little that they could do, with development policies and the budget largely set by the World Bank and the IMF. Indeed, Guebuza, who ran on a platform promising 'change' and often seemed to be running against Chissano rather than Dhlakama, seemed to be the only candidate to indicate a break with donor orthodoxy, when he suggested the need for a development bank. It would appear that Mozambicans have accepted Frelimo as the 'natural' party of government, rather like the ANC in neighbouring South Africa. There seems to be no serious political opposition on the horizon, and Mozambique appears to have become an *elected one-party state.*

Although the victory of Guebuza was clear and convincing, the election itself was widely condemned by international observers from the EU, Carter Center and the Commonwealth for *fraud, misconduct and incompetence.* The electoral register was a combination of 1999, 2003 and 2004 registrations and contained more than 11 m names (compared to a voting age population of 9.1 m), while computerisation of the register had been extremely sloppy (an example of the 'deixa andar' attitude that pervaded government) with many errors, omissions and duplications. After the 2003 local elections, the constitutional council ordered a clean-up, but only a rushed partial one was undertaken in the four months before the elections. The July registration update started late and missed many potential voters (especially in Renamo majority areas) because of lack of film for voters' photo cards and fuel for mobile brigades in rural areas.

The whole process was overshadowed by *the obsessive secrecy* of the National Election Commission (CNE). Former US President Jimmy Carter, who observed the election, said he had never seen anything like it in any election he had observed. Computer software for tabulating the results was written by CNE staff and kept secret. At the last minute, CNE ordered an audit of the software, which revealed major security lapses, including uncontrolled access to the database by senior election officials. The same thing had occurred in 1999, and no detailed results were ever published. In meetings with the press during the 2004 election, Carter raised questions about the 1999 results, and, in private, election staff admitted to using their computer access to tamper with results in that year. Discussions during 2004 made it clear that the actual results in 1999 must have been much closer than the official 200,000 votes victory margin for Chissano.

The *chaos in the voters' roll* and the confusion caused by the hasty rewriting of the tabulation software meant that an official list of polling stations was never published (CNE said it was 'a state secret') and the computer database contained at least 600 nonexistent polling stations. The counting system is complex. Each polling station has no more than 1,000 voters and the count is done in the polling station in the presence of party agents and observers. Results sheets are then posted at each polling station and sent to the provincial and national levels for tabulation. At national level, CNE then makes 'corrections' entirely in secret and with no explanation. Computer chaos meant hundreds of results sheets were rejected by the computers and had to be tabulated by hand. In addition, the constitutional council revealed that 699 presidential results sheets and 731 parliamentary results sheets – nearly 6% of all polling stations – were not counted in the final tally because the results sheets had simply been stolen or had ink poured over them.

Nor had the *voting process* gone smoothly. The 'Mozambique Political Process Bulletin' estimated that people at more than 700 polling stations were unable to vote because polling stations did not open or opened very late, because they were in the wrong place, or because they had the wrong register books. This seems to have particularly affected areas that had voted for Renamo in the past. Election commissions at provincial and local level also proved as partisan in many areas. More than 100 independent domestic observers were refused credentials and hundreds of Renamo party delegates were refused credentials or expelled from polling stations and often from entire districts by force. This allowed ballot box stuffing in at least 300 polling stations and probably accounted for at least 100,000 of the votes for Guebuza. In some of the polling stations there were turnouts of over 100% and nearly everyone voted for Guebuza. The ballot box stuffing did not change the presidential result, but cost Renamo at least three parliamentary seats.

The fraud and misconduct did not provoke a public response because two *parallel counts* based on results sheets posted at individual polling stations confirmed the landslide victory. The domestic Electoral Observatory did a simple sample count from every 16th polling station (as best as could be located without a full list of polling stations) and 200 Radio Mozambique reporters read out results from individual polling stations live on the air for two days, eventually covering half of all polling stations. By early on the first day after voting, Radio Mozambique had confirmed the low turnout and huge Frelimo majority.

Armando Guebuza promised *sweeping changes*, including an end to 'deixa andar' and curbs on corruption. The government had to be agreed upon with the Frelimo political commission and there was extensive negotiation between factions, as well as a need to protect some allegedly corrupt Chissano cronies. The two top posts went to women – Luisa Diogo remained as prime minister and political commission member Alcinda Abreu became foreign minister.

The new government is much less Maputo-focused. Guebuza in early speeches stressed the need to *prioritise development* outside the Maputo area, and he created a new development and planning ministry. All ten governors in the previous administration were given posts as ministers or deputy ministers, and several other ministers have strong grassroots links in either party or provincial government. The new government has the style of Samora Machel, with ministers making unannounced visits and expecting civil servants to arrive at work on time, at 7.30, and with public meetings in which people are encouraged to speak out and criticise and complain. Guebuza and Diogo also immediately challenged the IMF by ordering the hiring of 6,000 more teachers and presenting to parliament a budget that breaks spending limits. The biggest question remained over the justice system and the willingness of the new government to deal with corrupt members of the Frelimo elite.

On other political matters, *mayors and local assemblies* took office between 5 and 10 February, following elections the previous November. For the first time, the opposition Renamo party controlled four of 33 municipalities, including the port cities of Beira and Nacala. A *revised constitution* was approved at a special parliamentary session on 16 November. It makes no fundamental changes but slightly increases individual rights, allows dual nationality and changes contested wording to confirm that a president can serve only two five-year terms. The *justice* sector remains one of the biggest problems, with widespread corruption and inefficiency. For example, Supreme Court President Mario Mangaze reported that at the end of 2004 the supreme court had a backlog of 107,047 cases. At current rates, this will take more than four years to clear, but new cases are arising faster than old ones are dealt with. Corruption, combined with the huge backlog, make it very difficult to enforce contracts, and this is now seen as a major constraint on investment.

The *looting of two privatised state banks* in the late 1990s continues to cause ripples. It is widely believed that the main beneficiaries were people close to then President Joaquim Chissano. Two people who tried to investigate the matter, editor Carlos Cardoso and the head of banking supervision at the central bank, Siba-Siba Macuacua, were both assassinated. With the informal agreement of most of the donor community, Siba-Siba's murder was never investigated. Cardoso, however, had many friends abroad, and in 2003 six people who carried out the murder were convicted. The alleged leader of the hit squad, Anibal dos Santos Junior ('Anibalzinho') was twice allowed to escape from the high security prison: on 1 September 2002 (after which he was tried *in absentia* and then caught in South Africa in 2003 by a team from the public prosecutor's office operating without the knowledge of the interior ministry) and again on 9 May. He was caught on 24 May in Canada and deported back to Mozambique on 21 January 2005, after the supreme court unexpectedly and without clear explanation granted him a new trial. Meanwhile, on 15 June seven people were sentenced for fraud for taking $ 14 m from one of the banks in 1996: the investigation and trial had been repeatedly delayed, amid rumours that higher level people were involved.

Foreign Affairs

Mozambique remains highly fashionable with the *international donor community*, which continues to increase aid. It has become an important stop for foreign visitors. Mozambique is one of 16 countries eligible for the US Millennium Challenge Account: it has applied for $ 150 m but no decision had been reached. However, corruption continues to be an issue. Most donors were prepared to turn a blind eye, but the Nordic states were not. After an audit, *Sweden* demanded that the ministry of education repay $ 400,000 that had been misused, allegedly in part for scholarships for friends and family of the minister, and for failure to use proper tendering procedures.

The then Portuguese Prime Minister José Manuel Durão Barroso visited Mozambique on 28 March, but relations with *Portugal* were somewhat tense, in part because changes in the Portuguese government meant the breaking off of the long-running negotiations over the Cahora Bassa dam, which is still 82% owned by Portugal. Brazilian President Luis Inacio Lula da Silva had promised closer cooperation during a visit in late 2003, including plans to build a factory to produce anti-retroviral drugs. Chissano then visited *Brazil* from 31 August to 4 September. No progress was made on the ARV factory, but the Brazilian mining company Companhia do Vale do Rio Doce won a contract on 12 November to take over the Moatize coal mines, which have been largely inactive for more than 20 years. In return, it paid Mozambique $ 123 m and plans to export 13 m tonnes of coal a year to Brazil. *China* continues to build links with Mozambique. The Chinese constructed the headquarters for the foreign ministry, which were completed in 2004, and a Chinese company won the contract to expand the Maputo water system.

Mozambique's President Joaquim Chissano completed his one-year term as president of the *African Union* on 6 July. Because of his position, Mozambique hosted a series of international meetings. The NEPAD implementation committee met in Maputo on 23 May. Chissano was a speaker at the World Economic Forum at Davos, Switzerland on 23 January and on 2–4 June Maputo hosted the African Economic Summit, which is part of the World Economic Forum. The heads of state summit of the ACP partners of the EU took place in Maputo from 23 to 25 June. The summit's final statement was highly critical of the EU on a number of trade issues. And Prime Minister Luisa Diogo, in an opening speech, accused industrialised countries of "a lack of political will to attend to the genuine problems of the developing countries."

Mozambique had a contingent of 200 soldiers with UN forces in Burundi and sent observers to Darfur in Sudan. Mozambique has good relations with all its neighbouring states. *South Africa* has become an important investor and the South African presence is increasingly notable in the south of the country. President Joaquim Chissano and the government have backed Zimbabwean President *Robert Mugabe*, but have not said a great deal in public: Mozambique's leaders do not want to set a precedent for the overthrow of a long-standing leader. Privately, many in the Mozambican elite are fed up with kowtowing to donors and they respect Mugabe for standing up to Britain and the US.

Socioeconomic Developments

Economic growth was again expected to be over 8%, with inflation at 11%, according to the governor of the Bank of Mozambique, Adriano Maleiane. But commercial bank interest rates remained very high at 24%, which limited investment by those without access to credit outside Mozambique. The devaluation of the dollar (down 16% against the metical) helped keep inflation down, but caused problems for those export commodities priced in dollars, particularly cashew nuts and cotton.

Foreign investment remains high primarily in the minerals and energy sector, which generates income for Mozambique but, because of its largely enclave character, contributed little to development and employment creation. The *Mozal aluminium smelter*, one of the largest single private investment projects in Africa, is owned by the Australian company Billiton. It was located in Mozambique because of the port and access to cheap electricity from South Africa (actually imported at low prices from Cahora Bassa). Currently, the Mozal smelter produces 550,000 tonnes of aluminium per year, following the doubling of capacity that came on line in late 2003, but a second planned expansion project will raise this to 750,000 tonnes per year. Natural gas from an offshore field began to flow through a pipeline to South Africa on 26 March.

In October, the Irish Kenmare Resources began construction on a \$ 450 m *titanium mine* in Moma: the mine could add 2% to Mozambique's GDP but will create no more than 2,000 jobs. The Australian mining company WMC has rights to titanium in Chibuto, but the project has been delayed by the inability to negotiate a low enough electricity price with South Africa's Eskom.

Management of the central *railway* system from Beira port was won on 5 October by a company which is 51% an Indian consortium and 49% the Mozambican railways company CFM. It will operate the line to Beira and take control of the line to the Moatize coalmines and Malawi, which was destroyed by South African and Renamo forces during the war of destabilisation in the 1980s. On 16 December, the World Bank signed an agreement for a loan to provide \$ 104 m of the \$ 165 m needed to rehabilitate the railway to the Moatize coalmines, and the Indian partners will provide the rest of the rehabilitation money. Agreement has also been reached on management of the northern railway system linking the port of Nacala to Malawi. The consortium has Malawian, Mozambican, US, Portuguese and South African partners.

Sugar is the only productive sector to be protected by import tariffs, and one of the other two sectors to show substantial growth. Four sugar mills have been rehabilitated with investment from Mauritius and South Africa, and employment exceeds 20,000. But the industry is threatened by changed EU import policies, which may cut the high fixed import price and make the industry unprofitable. *Tobacco* production has jumped from 2,000 tonnes in 2000 to 45,000 tonnes, making it the sixth largest export (after aluminium, gas, prawns and fish, timber and sugar). Tobacco producers are mainly peasant out-growers, but also include a group of farmers expelled from land in Zimbabwe who moved across the border to Manica province.

Unemployment continues to rise. According to the National Statistics Institute Workforce Bulletin, formal sector employment is said to have been 301,000 in 2002, more than half in small enterprises. However, registered unemployment has risen steadily, from 109,000 at the end of 2000 to 140,000 at the end of 2004. *Telecommunications* is slowly being opened to competition. The first private mobile phone company, Vodacom, began operations and had by the end of the year 195,000 subscribers compared to 550,000 with the state-owned M-Cel (although many of those are pre-paid and relatively low use). This compares to 80,000 fixed lines with the state owned TDM. For the first time, there is serious private competition for the state-owned airline, LAM. Air Corridor, based in the northern city of Nampula, now links most major cities. All 128 district-capitals now have electricity, and the power line from Cahora Bassa is being extended and is expected to reach the two northern provincial capitals of Pemba and Lichinga in early 2005. Pemba's oil-fired power station suffered a disastrous fire on 26 December, resulting in serious power cuts.

An estimated 14.9% of Mozambicans between 15 and 49 years old are believed to be HIV positive and *AIDS* now accounts for 23% of all deaths, and an estimated 400,000 Mozambicans have died of the disease. The ministry of health estimates that 1.5 m Mozambicans are HIV positive and at least 200,000 with sufficiently advanced AIDS could benefit from anti-retroviral therapy. By contrast, only 6,500 people were receiving anti-retroviral drugs by the end of the year and the number was planned to rise to only 20,000 during 2005. Spending on HIV/AIDS now exceeds $ 50 m per year. *Malaria* remains the other big disease problem, the ministry of health reported in April. There were 4.5 m cases in 2003, leading to 3,212 deaths in hospital and many more who died without being counted in rural areas.

Confusion remains about whether ordinary Mozambicans are better off and have gained from the high GDP growth rates. Data published in 2004 by the National Statistics Institute cover only through 2002, and show that, despite rapid rises in GDP, *per capita consumption* is actually falling from a high of $ 199 in 1998 to $ 146 in 2002 – the same level as at the end of the war of destabilisation in 1992. On 30 March, the government published its 2002–03 household survey, which showed that Mozambicans living below the local extreme poverty lines fell from 69% in 1997 to 54% in 2003. Income gaps are huge: the bottom 10% of the population accounts for only 2% of expenditure and the bottom 50% accounts for only 21%, while at the top the richest 20% accounts for 53% of expenditure and the top 10% spends 39%.

On 21 May, the national statistics institute and UNICEF jointly released new data based on a *demographics and health* survey. These show 41% of all children under five suffer from chronic malnutrition. Under-five mortality has improved substantially, falling from 263 per 1,000 live births in 1997 to 178 in 2003. Maputo city has the lowest poverty and under-five mortality, while Cabo Delgado in the north is worst. Access to safe drinking water remains low, increasing from 36% to 40% of the population over the last four years, according to Deputy Water Minister Jenrique Cossa. Adult (aged 15 and above) illiteracy fell from over 90% at independence in 1975 to 60% in the 1997 census to 54% in the 2002–03 family survey but education remains only a dream for many children – there are one million children between 6 and 13 who cannot get a place in primary school.

On 16 April, the government increased the *minimum wage* by 14% to meticais 1,120,297 (then $ 46.7) per month. The minimum wage has increased steadily, and faster than inflation, since 1996, when it was $ 23.7. The agricultural minimum wage was increased to $ 33.6. Removing *landmines* planted during the 1964–74 liberation war and the 1976–92 war of destabilisation continues: it was announced on 2 November that 220 m square metres had been cleared since 1996, at a cost of $ 189 m. However, corruption in the de-mining programme caused delays. Over 177,000 weapons have been destroyed over a nine-year period in joint Mozambican-South African police operations. Mozambique retains one of the smallest armies in the region and there is a strong bias against military service. Registration is compulsory for all 18 year-olds, but in January fewer than 10% actually registered.

A new *family law* was approved by parliament on 24 August, which in general improves the status of women. In addition to civil marriages, the law recognises traditional and religious marriages and de facto unions, which in particular means that a man is responsible for paying maintenance for his children and former partner. *Radio* remains the main source of information in the country, predominantly the government-owned Radio Moçambique (RM) and 'Televisão Moçambique' (TVM), which broadcast in all languages and from all provincial capitals, although there are now a number of private television and radio stations. The family survey published during the year showed that 50% of households had access to a radio, compared to 27% in the 1997 census. The Mozambican *print media* remains small but lively, competitive and free. The state-owned daily, 'Notícias', prints 13,000 copies per day, and it owns the Sunday newspaper 'Domingo' (circulation 10,000) as well as the sports weekly 'Desáfio' (4,000), so that the company is profitable. The private Beira-based daily 'Diário de Moçambique' has a circulation of 5,000. There are four private weeklies: 'Savana' (14,000), 'Zabeze' (6,000), 'Demos' (2,000) and 'Embondeiro'. In addition, there were several Maputo-based faxed dailies and various local newspapers and community radios, largely supported by donor funds.

Mozambique in 2005

The new president spent most of the year trying to gain control over the state machine, as resistance to change proved much fiercer than expected. The result was few new policies or initiatives. The economy continued to grow at more than 7%, but concern increased at the lack of rural development. Mozambique continued to be the donor darling, with promises of increased aid flows.

Domestic Politics

In the first non-violent *handover of presidential power*, Armando Guebuza of Frelimo took office on 2 February. The 62-year old Guebuza was, like his predecessors Joaquim Chissano and Samora Machel, a veteran of the liberation war, so this is not a generation change. However, he promised to rebuild the party, end corruption and give dynamism to the government. Guebuza's victory in the 1–2 December 2004 election was clear and convincing, but the election itself was heavily criticised by international observers for fraud, misconduct, incompetence and obsessive secrecy.

Similar problems dogged a by-election for mayor of the small town of Mocimboa da Praia on 21 May. The Frelimo candidate won by 533 votes, but observers found that about 300 votes for the opposition candidate had been improperly excluded. Protests followed, including a demonstration by 90 naked Renamo members on 20 July. Then in *violent clashes* on 4–5 September, at least eight people were killed.

Meanwhile, the ad hoc parliamentary commission to revise the electoral law remained stalemated during the year. The *council of*

 | DOI 10.1163/9789004301122_003

state, which is called for in the constitution that took effect in January, was sworn in on 23 December. The president must consult the council on the holding of elections, declarations of war and for general advice. It includes the president, prime minister, speaker of parliament, past presidents and speakers, the head of the opposition and other prominent people appointed by the two main parties.

Guebuza put great emphasis on *rebuilding the Frelimo party*, not just as an electoral machine but also as the dominant political force in the country. The party has returned to the custom of calling members 'comrade' and there are growing complaints that it is easier for 'comrades' to receive assistance, licences, contracts, etc. from the government. One incident occurred in the municipality of Ilha de Moçambique, where the Renamo opposition had won the local elections in 2003. All technical staff from the town council were removed from the municipality by central government and transferred to other posts in the province. Another occurred in December, when the Manica provincial court ruled that the local government had been acting improperly by blocking Renamo from constructing a headquarters in Guro.

Guebuza is also trying to tighten his *control over the party*, and the next party congress has been brought forward to late 2006. Frelimo is notable for having remained united for more than 35 years, with no splits and few expulsions. The fact that the party is seen as more important than any individual is one reason that Mozambique has not gone in for the highly personalised direction of Uganda and Zimbabwe, and is instead more like South Africa and Tanzania. Chissano, despite being bitter at having been rejected by the party, still campaigned for Guebuza. However, keeping the party together also exacts a high price – there are major internal divisions and the interests of party barons must be satisfied, which also includes tolerance of significant corruption.

Guebuza had to reach agreement on his government with the Frelimo Political Commission and this involved extensive horse-trading. Chissano remains a force in the party and his allies kept control over the justice system (ensuring that it remains weak and politicised and that corrupt members of the elite are not prosecuted) while the interior ministry is now headed by a Guebuza man who is trying to clean the Stygian stables of a police force linked to organised crime and also involved in petty corruption. The ministry of planning and finance was split, with a ministry of finance headed by a Chissano ally and a new ministry of planning and development headed by a Guebuza protégé.

Virtually all ministers were changed (with the notable exception of Prime Minister Luisa Diogo, who is acceptable to all factions within the party and is popular with donors) and the *new government* is political and managerial rather than technocratic – most ministers started with little knowledge of their ministry subject. Cabinet members are also younger and better educated: several ministers had studied for degrees at night, by correspondence, or part time and they come from the first generation to benefit from the rapid post-independence expansion of education. All 10 of the Chissano-appointed governors were elevated to ministerial or vice-ministerial posts. Initially, Guebuza and his ministers adopted the style of Samora Machel 20 years earlier of issuing orientations and expecting that state apparatus to jump to attention and make changes. This did not happen. Much publicised promises for the first 100 days were quickly forgotten.

The *clean broom attitude* of the new government meant that all actions of the previous government were reviewed or simply discarded. Ministers' distrust of their own inherited staff led them to ignore technical advice and to rapidly centralise decision making, resulting in ministers simply being overwhelmed. There had been widespread abuse of cars, travel and mobile telephones so some ministers simple recalled the cars and stopped mobile phone use and travel, causing on-going projects to grind to a halt and ending vital central supervision of provincial activities. Mistrust and lack of experience led to confusion and lack of direction.

At the same time, there had not been a thorough going reform of government since changes introduced at independence. Thus Guebuza faced an *entrenched bureaucracy* that had never been forced to rethink its ways of doing things. Fiefdoms had been created that sheltered comfortable ways of doing things, as people saw no reason to change when the system seemed to run well, but people also feared a loss of power. And the system sheltered widespread corruption through myriad loan funds, contracts and opportunities for bribery and patronage. The result was that the bureaucracy dug in its heels and resisted all change. The first six months were characterised by total gridlock and resistance. Even by year's end, some ministries had not been fully reorganised and some civil servants were still not sure what department they were in.

Two incidents illustrated the open *challenges to change*. Interior Minister Jose Pacheco had struggled to gain control of his ministry. The director of the Maputo central prison was gunned down on 21 October, apparently because he tried to reduce the control of organised crime over the prisons, and there have been several important prison break-outs. Finally, on 30 December, when most people had already gone on holiday, Pacheco called a press conference to say that an audit of the ministry showed that $ 9 m could not be accounted from the term of his predecessor, and Chissano loyalist, Almerino Manhenje. Pacheco said criminal proceedings would be initiated. No one expected to see Manhenje in the dock, but it was a clear warning – one year into the new government – for the Chissano and organised crime groups to stop their obstruction of change in the ministry of interior. The other incident came after Pedro Taímo was dismissed as labour ministry delegate in South Africa and his office sealed. In an unprecedented action, Taímo went public and gave a series of interviews objecting to his sacking. He stressed the services he had undertaken for past governments, said the minister had taken a "suicidal" decision and blamed it all on "tribalism" in the new government.

Justice remains a particular problem. The supreme court president, Mário Mangaze, admitted that there were 103,653 cases pending in the courts at the end of 2005 and that only 40,000 cases had been judged during the year. He also said that during the previous decade, only 42 judges had been punished for misconduct.

On the other hand, Guebuza's *emphasis on development* has led to a series of initiatives. In his inaugural speech on 2 February, Guebuza promised special attention to technical and vocational training "in order to meet the needs of local and national development", and the new Education Minister Aires Aly later announced a new stress on technical education. A new ministry of science and technology was created, with an active minister, Venancio Massingue. And with the rising price of oil, there was a move to develop bio-fuels and use local natural gas as fuel for cars. On an administrative level, the new government introduced the concept of permanent secretaries, not just in ministries but also in provincial and district administrations. As part of a new push for decentralisation, the 2006 budget gives each district $ 280,000 to spend on locally determined projects. Guebuza toured the country and made repeated speeches calling on all citizens to fight poverty and corruption. In a speech on independence day (25 June), he called on all citizens to struggle against "the obstacles to development", which include "the spirit of apathy and drift, red tape, corruption and crime". On 12 October, he urged Mozambicans to believe that they can defeat poverty, just as it was possible to defeat colonialism and win independence in 1975 and just as it was possible to end the war in 1992.

The man who led the team responsible for the *killing of Carlos Cardoso* on 22 November 2000 was tried and convicted for a second time. Anibal dos Santos Junior (Anibalzinho) had twice been allowed to escape from the 'maximum security' prison in Maputo. The first time was during the trial of the killers and Anibalzinho was found guilty in absentia. He was captured in South Africa and returned to Mozambique, only to escape again to Canada. On 21 December 2004, the Mozambican supreme court issued an unexpected ruling that Anibalzinho had the right to be present at the trial. He was deported to Mozambique on 21 January and he was jailed in a special cell in the Maputo city police command. The trial resumed on 2 December. In her final statement on 19 December, Lucinda Cruz, the lawyer for the Cardoso family, said that Anibalzinho had "powerful protection", which must be investigated. She noted that Anibalzinho renounced his Mozambican nationality so that he would not have to do military service, yet he was allowed to stay in Mozambique for another decade, despite having no job and being arrested several times. Notwithstanding the existence of two arrest warrants, no attempt was made to detain or expel him. "Who protects him, allowing him to commit crimes continually, with arrest warrants never served, even though his usual residence is well known?" Cruz asked. He was finally arrested after the Cardoso murder, but was twice able to escape. Cruz said that "what is most strange" was that Anibalzinho was willing to incriminate himself in the crime, yet went out of his way to proclaim the innocence of the family of then President Joaquim Chissano, especially his son Nhimpine Chissano, as well as the Mozambican government and the Frelimo party. "Why was he obsessed with defending these people and entities?" Cruz asked.

Foreign Affairs

Mozambique and Portugal unexpectedly reached a deal on the *Cahora Bassa dam* on 2 November during Guebuza's first official visit as president to the former colonial power. Built during the colonial era to supply electricity to South Africa, it was never profitable because Portugal agreed a very low electricity tariff in exchange for military support against the Frelimo guerrillas. Because this agreement was binding for many years into the future, Frelimo refused to accept the dam at independence, so it remained 82% Portuguese government-owned and 18% Mozambican government-owned. Debts rose to $ 2.3 bn. Mozambique was increasingly anxious to take control of the dam not only on nationalist grounds, but also because it needs control of the dam before it can build another dam downstream from Cahora Bassa. Meanwhile, Portugal was coming under increasing pressure from the EU to cut its deficit. Consequently, Portugal agreed to sell all but 15% of the dam if Mozambique would pay $ 950 m during 2006.

Improved relations with neighbours were high on the agenda, and an abolition of visas was agreed with South Africa, Botswana, Zambia, Tanzania and Swaziland. Visas with Malawi had already been abolished. On 15 October, Guebuza and Tanzanian President Benjamin Mkapa laid the first stone of the Unity Bridge across the Rovuma River, which forms their border. Mozambique is a signatory to the SADC free trade agreement, which involves a steady reduction of tariffs to reach zero in 2012 for all countries except South Africa, which will reach zero in 2015. Mozambique had 40,000 miners in South Africa, down from 55,000 in 1996.

Former President Joaquim Chissano is playing an *increasing international role*. On 29 April he was appointed a special envoy to Guinea-Bissau by UN Secretary-General Kofi Annan and on

17 October he was appointed an advisor to UNCTAD. Mozambique continues to send peacekeeping troops to Burundi. The fourth contingent of 180 served during the second half of the year: four were killed in a road accident.

China is playing an increasing role in Mozambique. Chinese contractors have won about one-third of the international tenders for road building and they are participating in the rehabilitation and extension of water systems in three big cities. In general, Chinese tender prices are 25% cheaper than others, but there are few linkages to the Mozambican economy. China has also invested in several joint ventures.

Two senior Mozambicans called for increased *South-South cooperation* in major speeches – Prime Minister Luisa Diogo at the Asia-Africa summit on 23 April and President Armando Guebuza on 15 June at the Group of 77 summit in Doha. And in a speech on 1 June at the African Economic Forum, he called on leaders of industrialised nations to back up their fine words and promises with more practical action: "We have heard many promises from them, but now is the time to move from words to deeds, and give what Africa really needs to develop, which is mainly financial and technological resources."

Mozambique remains highly fashionable with the *international donors*, which continue to increase aid. In 2004, Mozambique received $ 1.2 bn in aid, of which $ 209 m was technical cooperation, $ 72 m was food and emergency aid and $ 21 m was debt relief. However, the remaining $ 898 m was money Mozambique could use, and more than one-third, $ 333 m, went as *budget support*. Mozambique has become one of the most important test beds for direct support to the state budget, and 18 donors together fund one-fifth of the government budget. These donors formed a group known as Programme Aid Partnership (PAP) and on 12–13 May they met with government and an agreed *aide-memoire* was published. This is an apparently unique joint donor-government process, which has involved an exceptional degree of collaboration among donors themselves and between donors and government, as well as an unprecedented degree of transparency. The process is immensely complex. There were 23 working groups, which involved perhaps 200 people from donor and government sides who worked intensively over two months before the meeting. The reports are nearly all public. The agreed *aid-memoire* has 134 detailed 'recommendations' to be carried out by government and donors over the next year, plus a Performance Assessment Framework (PAF). A joint donor-government statement issued on 12 May said Mozambique failed to meet almost all of its targets for governance, justice or corruption control set in 2004, but its performance over the past year was still "satisfactory". The report also criticised the government for "substantially" under-spending its budgets for poverty reduction, noting that the percentage of spending on "priority sectors" actually fell between 2003 and 2004.

Perhaps most unusually, *donor performance* was also evaluated, both in the *aide-memoire* and in a specially commissioned independent study 'Perfect Partners?' by Tony Killick, Carlos Castel-Branco and Richard Gerster. On the donor side, the *aide-memoire* says "weaknesses are most pronounced in the area of transparency". Only a few donors complied with government reporting requirements and donors have failed in attempts to reduce the government's administrative burden. For example, there were 143 donor missions in 2004 involving 16 of the budget support donors, not counting the World Bank, which was unwilling to say how many missions there were. There is also a problem that aid flows remain late and unpredictable. The 'Perfect Partners?' report says: "A large proportion of total assistance coming into the country is made up of a multitude of uncoordinated, often donor-driven, development and technical assistance projects, which do not add up to a coherent whole, do not necessarily promote the GoM's [Government of Mozambique's] priorities and of which the GoM has incomplete knowledge."

It calls on the government to "turn down low-priority offers of 'assistance' [and] be willing to say 'no' to donors promoting their pet projects and schemes". Having castigated the donors, the Killick report is especially critical of the government for being "passive", for "weak" leadership and for lack of involvement, both at central and sectoral levels. The government was "hardly involved" in setting up the first Performance Assessment Framework in 2004. "We are uneasy about the extent to which the PAPPA [Programme Aid Partners Performance Assessment] processes are seen as largely matters for the donors, with the GoM somewhat passive".

Apparently the government feels its aid dependence "means it is not in a position to insist on its priorities", the Killick report continues. "We would like to stress that aid dependency does not have to entail subservience and that boldness by the government can go part way to redressing the asymmetry". The *reluctance to criticise donors* was shown in the issue of a development bank. Mozambique is one of the few countries not to have such a bank and it was part of Guebuza's election programme. However, the donor community was totally hostile and began secret meetings to block the bank. An angry Guebuza finally used a speech on 9 December at the Carter Center in Atlanta, far from home, to criticise the donors for blocking the government on the bank and for not letting Mozambique set its own development priorities. The *US Millennium Challenge Corporation* failed to agree on money for Mozambique, despite demanding disproportionate amounts of time from government staff. Privately, government officials accused the US agency of time wasting and, by trying to start from scratch and re-invent the aid wheel, of using working methods that had been discredited 20 years ago.

Donors have tended to give only lip service to curbing *corruption*, but two donors responded to corruption in the ministry of education. Sweden demanded that stolen money be repaid, while Denmark cut aid to education. A confrontation was avoided when the government finally agreed to the forensic audit of Banco Austral that had been demanded by donors for more than two years. The privatised bank went bankrupt with several hundred million dollars in bad debts, many involving the Frelimo elite. The head of banking supervision for the central bank, Siba Siba Macuacua, was assassinated when he tried to investigate the frauds, but the murder has never been investigated.

International management *contracts for two key railway lines* proved problematic. The government said it was not satisfied with the work undertaken by the US-based consortium managing the Nacala railway and port in the north, and on 2 November announced it had cancelled the contract with the South African rail company Spoornet to manage the Maputo-South Africa line. However, the Indian-led consortium running the central railway to the port of Beira has been more successful and the World Bank released $ 130 m for rehabilitation of a line destroyed in the war of destabilisation in the 1980s and never reopened.

Socioeconomic Developments

Economic growth was again over 7%, but *inflation* hit 14%, well above the planned 8% and the 2004 level of 9.3%, according to the national statistics institution.

Because elections were not held until December 2004, the budget and plan for 2005 were not presented until March, but the budget and plan for 2006 were approved on schedule by parliament on 16 and 20 December. The budget for 2006 is $ 1.9 bn,

27% of GDP. Of this 47% will be covered by government revenue and 53% by donors and World Bank loans. Exactly two-thirds of the budget goes to priority areas for poverty reduction, including \$ 376 m for education, \$ 300 m each for health and infrastructure and \$ 60 m for agriculture and rural development. By contrast, military expenditure is about \$ 30 m.

Mozambique is unlikely to meet most of the *Millennium Development Goals*, according to a joint UN-government report published in August. It is "unlikely" to meet education or environment goals. It is "unlikely" to halt the spread of HIV/AIDS by 2015 but can "potentially" have begun to reduce the incidence of malaria by that date. It can "potentially" meet the goals for child and maternal mortality. It can "potentially" halve the number of people living in extreme poverty by 2015 but is "unlikely" to halve the proportion of people who suffer from malnutrition. The report notes that 24% of children under five years old are underweight and that this situation is not improving. Only 40% of Mozambicans have access to safe water, Public Works Minister Felicio Zacarias said on 25 November. Less than half the population has access to health centres, Health Minister Ivo Garrido said on 21 November: only 47% of births take place in health units.

Malaria remains the biggest killer, accounting for 60% of hospital admissions and 30% of hospital deaths, the ministry of health coordinating council said on 7 June. Spraying in an area in the south reduced the number of cases by up to 75%, but is too expensive to extend nation-wide. *HIV/AIDS* is a growing problem. The latest statistics presented by Health Minister Garrido were from 2004. Data from sentinel sites indicates that 16.2% of Mozambicans aged between 15 and 49 are HIV positive. An estimated 800,000 women, 570,000 men and 80,000 children were HIV positive and 97,000 people died of AIDS-related causes. The minister predicted that by 2010, 15% of health workers and 9,200 teachers will have died of AIDS. On 18 November, the commander of the police, Miguel dos Santos, said that 500 to 600 policemen a year were dying of AIDS. *Antiretroviral treatment* had reached 20,000 people by the end of the year – less than 10% of those with advanced AIDS who could benefit. Women's Minister Virgilia Matabele disclosed that 380,000 children had lost one or both parents to the disease. Matabele also stressed the *feminisation of the epidemic*, noting that of 130,000 teenagers believed to be HIV positive, 75% were girls.

The government budget for HIV/AIDS was $ 54 m. However, the 12–13 May joint government-donor *aide-memoire* was caustic about the government's HIV/AIDS programme. "The national response is still not commensurate with the scale of the epidemic... The development and implementation of sectoral HIV strategies has been negligible. In addition, the national HIV response has suffered from a lack of strong political leadership at all levels and across all sectors."

The board that is supposed to lead the HIV/AIDS programme did not even meet the year before.

The *aide-memoire* also criticised the government for lack of attention to *gender equality* in official documents such as the PARPA (the Poverty Reduction Strategy Paper), budget and plan. "None of the sectors has progressed much in institutionalising and mainstreaming gender. Gender inequalities are evident in primary education indicators; the health sector information systems cannot provide data to measure gender disparities; and gender inequality is one of the driving forces behind the HIV/AIDS epidemic."

Natural gas from the Pande field had begun flowing to South Africa and a branch pipeline opened that serves some industry in southern Mozambique. The government intends to introduce natural-gas powered vehicles. Meanwhile, it signed a contract for gas prospecting in two blocks adjoining Pande and opened tenders for oil prospecting in the Rovuma basin in the north. There has been repeated oil exploration over several decades, but no oil has been found yet.

In the colonial era, Mozambique's road and railway system was largely designed to link the British colonies and South Africa to Mozambican ports. There was never even a complete *north-south road*. Work finally began on an $ 80 m bridge across the Zambezi River. When completed, it will plug a major gap, play an important political role in national unity and should also increase trade between the north and south of the country.

Removal of mines from three different wars continues. On 8 June, Foreign Minister Alcinda Abreu reported that during 2004 nearly 100,000 mines and other items of unexploded ordnance were located and destroyed, freeing 379 villages and 217,000 people from the threat of mines. However, people were still being killed and injured in land mine incidents and 204 villages with 806,000 people remained to be de-mined. More than a decade after the end of the war, the *anti-militarism* of Mozambican youth remains clear. Under Mozambican law, everyone who turns 18 must register for possible military service. During the January and February registration period, fewer than 10% of 18-year-olds actually registered.

Drought hit central Mozambique as well as neighbouring states. At first the government response was to deny the seriousness of the problem, and it required articles in the state-owned newspapers 'Notícias' and 'Domingo' highlighting the drought's severity to prod ministers into action. More than 1.2 m people were affected and at least 50 people died of starvation.

Mozambique will adopt a *new metical* as its currency. There are about 25,000 old meticais to the US dollar, and the new metical simply drops the last three zeros. This will simplify accounting, cash registers, petrol pumps, etc. and follows common custom where people don't mention 1000s in normal conversation. The law passed on 24 December stated that prices must be shown in new and old meticais for a year and that new and old notes and coins will both circulate.

Mozambique in 2006

Mozambique remains the donor darling, with aid rising. The economy continues to grow at more than 7% a year, but concern increases about the lack of rural development and Mozambique's inability to reach the MDGs. It was a politically quiet year with few changes.

Domestic Politics

Frelimo's 9th congress in Quelimane (11–15 November) produced few dramatic changes. Frelimo is no longer the party of workers and peasants: more than half the congress delegates worked for the party or the state. Of 1,326 delegates, only 90 were subsistence peasants and just 9 were industrial workers. Only 20 said they were members of the trade union federation OTM ('Organização dos Trabalhadores de Moçambique'), while 48 were business people. In contrast, 470 delegates worked in the state apparatus (183 teachers and 27 nurses) and 276 were in the Frelimo party apparatus. President Armando Guebuza consolidated his leadership but ex-President Joaquim Chissano remained a major force in the party and was elected honorary president. Some old-timers have been pensioned off and replaced by younger, better educated people, but the liberation movement generation remained a powerful force. The total openness and smooth running of the congress suggested that the sharp tensions between the various groups inside the party were successfully managed. Prime Minister Luísa Diogo proved to be the brightest rising star. In elections for the central committee, she came second with 1,105 votes, 33 votes behind Alberto Chipande (1138 votes), who fired the first shots

 | DOI 10.1163/9789004301122_004

of the liberation war in 1964, and ahead of Graça Machel (1,084 votes). Diogo must now be seen as a serious presidential candidate in 2014 (when Guebuza cannot stand again): at the time of the central committee elections she was 48 years old, compared to 61 for Graça Machel.

The *Political Commission* met almost weekly and set government policy. Next to Guebuza, Chissano and Chipande it includes five ministers – Diogo, Aiuba Cuereneia (development and planning), Aires Aly (education), Alcinda Abreu (foreign) and José Pacheco (interior) – as well as Maputo Mayor Eneas Comiche and the speaker of parliament, Eduardo Mulémbwè. Former Nampula provincial Governor Filipe Paunde was elected unopposed as secretary-general and is also a member of the Political Commission.

In April, the eldest son of former President Joaquim Chissano was formally charged with ordering the *murder of Carlos Cardoso*, Mozambique's best investigative journalist, in 2000. Nyimpine Chissano has also been charged with various economic offences. Initially, Albano Silva, the lawyer husband of Prime Minister Luísa Diogo, was the surprise choice as defence lawyer, but he had to step down as he had been a witness in a related case.

Three *elections* are due in the coming three years: 2007 for new provincial parliaments, 2008 for municipal assemblies and 2009 national elections for president and parliament. An ad hoc parliamentary commission began work on new election laws in March 2005 but ad hoc commissions require unanimity, so it was hamstrung by demands from the opposition party Renamo that it must be able to veto any decision by an election commission, and that the ad hoc commission could not consider any other issue unless this was granted. On 15 June, parliament remitted the laws to a standing commission, with normal voting. The new laws were approved in parliament on 20 December. Despite substantial concessions to Renamo, the opposition staged a noisy protest and stormed the speaker's table in an attempt to prevent a vote.

The *new election laws* largely maintained the present electoral system, with some important changes. The national elections commission, CNE ('Comissão Nacional de Eleições'), was reduced from 19 to 13 members – three Frelimo, two Renamo and eight nominated by civil society and chosen by parliament, so Frelimo is guaranteed a majority. Elections will be on one day rather than two. Mozambique has proven unable to update its electoral roll, so there will be a new registration every five years, for each electoral cycle. Presidential candidates will be required to submit a nomination petition of 10,000 names (as at present) and a $ 4,000 deposit. The 5% threshold for parliamentary elections is removed, which may permit small parties to gain seats. In national elections, only registered parties can stand, but in parliamentary and local elections independent citizens' lists will be allowed. The new election law did not, however, end the secrecy of the national count, which had been heavily criticised by international and national observers as well as Mozambique's own constitutional council. In past elections, the CNE made significant changes to the results without any public explanation.

In a radical shift, the administration of the *civil service* was split. A national public service authority, ANFP ('Autoridade Nacional da Função Pública'), sworn in on 11 July was made responsible for both national and provincial civil servants. The ministry of state administration, which previously had been responsible for all government employees, will only be responsible for districts and lower levels. The ANFP is headed by Victória Dias Diogo, former permanent secretary of tourism and sister of the prime minister, Luísa Diogo.

President Armando Guebuza continued to tour the country regularly, giving speeches in which he stated that it was possible to overcome poverty and underdevelopment. He put great stress on decentralisation. Each district was given a special budget of $ 280,000 per year to be spent on locally determined economic development projects. Consultative councils are being established at district and community level, while the national government is attempting to increase the number of skilled people in district governments. In his speeches, he emphasised the need for a change in attitude – for local people to believe that it is possible to overcome poverty and to take the initiative and not wait for central government.

Foreign Affairs

Mozambique remains a *donor darling*: aid continued to rise, from $ 1,246 m in 2004 to $ 1,285 m in 2005 (announced by DAC in January 2007). Aid is one-fifth of GDP and half of the government budget. Mozambique receives 50% more aid per capita than its neighbours Tanzania and Malawi. "Mozambique is a success story in Sub-Saharan Africa" wrote the IMF in a report on 1 December.

With an estimated 60 bilateral and multilateral donors and 150 international non-government organiations, the *bureaucracy* became increasingly complex. In a report for the British department for international development, the Mozambican academic Elisio Macamo wrote in June that the "regular review exercises, working groups, and high and middle level meetings between Government... officials and donors... may be necessary to reassure donors [but] consultation mechanisms appear to have become an end in itself." Government lacks people and time to fully participate, while "donors themselves have not always been able to prepare themselves adequately for these various meetings."

More than one-quarter of aid goes directly into the government budget, but this has increased rather than decreased the administrative burden. The 18 *budget support donors* have created an extremely cumbersome procedure for working with the government. To agree on goals for the coming year and assess performance in the past year, 24 working groups involved hundreds of donor and government staff during two months. Some very senior government officials did little other work in that period. At a press conference on 13 April, the minister for planning and development complained about the number of sleepless nights for his staff in the weeks before the meeting, while the Swedish ambassador, whose embassy led the donor side, admitted she was shocked by the amount of work involved. There was a time-consuming mid-term evaluation in October, which occupied people for a month.

The Confederation of Mozambican Business Associations (CTA) is totally dependent on USAID, which pays 93% of its expenses, the CTA revealed on 21 July.

Ireland is one of the budget support donors and President Mary McAleese visited on 14 June. *British* Chancellor of the Exchequer Gordon Brown visited on 10 April and promised extra aid for education. Guebuza visited London on 4–5 December. Economist and US special advisor Jeffrey Sachs visited in June: Mozambique is to have 11 of Sachs's special *millennium villages*. These are to be model villages on which $ 110 per person per year is spent.

Mozambique is taking control of the *Cahora Bassa dam*, following an agreement signed by President Armando Guebuza and Portuguese Prime Minister Jose Socrates in Maputo on 31 October, just a year after the deal was agreed in principle. Mozambique will buy two-thirds of the dam for $ 950 m, raising its share of 'Hidroeléctrica de Cahora Bassa' (HCB) from 18% to 85%. Mozambique is paying $ 700 m and refuses to say how it has raised the money. The other $ 250 m comes from profits of HCB itself. The delay in signing the Cahora Bassa deal occurred because Eurostat, the EU's independent statistical agency, initially refused to accept it. Portugal was under heavy EU pressure because of its large budget deficit, and it hoped the $ 950 m would partly plug the hole. But Portugal had claimed that HCB owed the Portuguese treasury over $ 2 bn, so Eurostat wanted Portugal to treat the deal as a $ 1 bn loss, which would worsen rather than help the Portuguese budget deficit.

Mozambique refused to take the dam at independence in 1975 because Portugal had agreed to sell electricity to apartheid South Africa at a loss in exchange for support for its colonial wars, which meant the dam would have been a drain on the Mozambican economy. Cahora Bassa is the highest dam in Africa and second largest in Africa by volume of water held (after Lower Usuma in Nigeria) and by hydroelectricity production (after Aswan in Egypt). Cahora Bassa can generate 2,075 megawatts and is running at 95% of capacity, selling 1,100 megawatts to South Africa, 450 megawatts to Zimbabwe and the rest to Mozambique. Ownership is particularly important because Mozambique wants to build *a second dam* at Mpanda Ncua, 70 km downstream: it would use the same water and thus the two dams would need to be managed together. Mpanda Nuca would generate 1,200 megawatts and cost $ 2.3 bn: funding was offered by China's Export Import Bank on 20 April. This is further linked to a proposal for an 1,800 megawatt coal-fired power station associated with the nearby Moatize coal mine, which has been privatised to a Brazilian firm 'Companhia do Vale do Rio Doce'.

President Guebuza has strongly defended African links with *China*, for example in a speech at Davos on 26 January. China is heavily involved in central Mozambique, where it is negotiating agriculture projects in the Zambesi valley. It will also build a new national stadium in Maputo, it announced on 18 November. A Chinese company is carrying out the project to expand the Maputo city water system. Guebuza went to China and met Chinese President Hu Jintao on 4 November. But there was controversy in December when a study revealed extensive illegal exports of timber to China.

Privatisation of the northern railway system and Maputo port has proved problematic, and on 23 March the chairman of the national ports and railways company said the new operators were not living up to their contracts. In particular, they were failing to make the promised investment. The northern railway was privatised to a US company because of continued US military interest in the deepwater port of Nacala. Rebuilding of the central railway system by an Indian leaseholder, with World Bank money, progressed rapidly, but the crisis in Zimbabwe cut traffic along one branch of the railway and through the port of Beira.

In July, Mozambique set up its national commission to participate in the *APRM*. Prime Minister Luísa Diogo was co-chair of the UN secretary-general's high-level panel on *UN system-wide coherence* in areas of development, humanitarian assistance and environment, which reported on 9 November. President Guebuza addressed the UN General Assembly on 21 September. The first meeting of the former heads of state club, the *Africa Forum*, was held in Maputo on 11 January. Former President Joaquim Chissano organised the meeting of 16 former heads of state.

Socioeconomic Developments

Inflation for 2006 was just under 10%, above the target of 7.5%, and economic growth was 7.8%. *Aid* and loans account for half the state budget. Military spending is only 2% of the government budget while education is 22% and health 12%: 526 new schools were built in 2006.

HIV/AIDS is a serious problem and by the end of the year 38,000 patients were receiving antiretroviral (ARV) drugs, out of 250,000 who needed them. In early 2006, donors criticised the government for not doing enough about AIDS, and the number of centres providing ARVs increased from 46 in June to 150 by the end of the year. The target for 2007 is 96,000 people on ARVs. It is estimated that more than 16% of Mozambicans between 15 and 49 years of age are infected and that 97,000 have already died. Life expectancy has fallen to 38 years, compared to an expected 46 without AIDS. About 1.5 m are infected – 800,000 women, 570,000 men and 80,000 children. In a speech on 15 March, Health Minister Dr. Ivo Garrido said that 15% of health workers and 9,000 teachers would die of AIDS by 2010. At least 380,000 children have lost one or both parents to AIDS. Linked to this is a growing tuberculosis epidemic. *Malaria* remains the second main cause of death, and is on the increase: 4,985 died of malaria compared to 4,209 the previous year.

Mozambique's new *poverty reduction strategy paper* (PARPA II, 'Plano de Acção para a Redução da Pobreza Absoluta, 2006–09', Action Plan to Reduce Absolute Poverty, 2006–09) was approved by the council of ministers on 2 May. It was negotiated with donors but was not presented to parliament. It puts more stress on the economy than the previous one and directs attention away from the social sectors, but it still largely follows the neo-liberal Washington Consensus line that it is for the private sector to develop the country and end poverty. It says "the function of the private sector is to grow the economy" and create jobs. "The success of the private sector depends on the functioning of the market economy, which, in large measure, depends on the force and quality of the private sector itself." The role of government is largely seen as creating a good business environment, improving 'human capital' through health and education, and building infrastructure such as roads and electricity.

UNDP released its Mozambique national human development report for 2005 on 6 September, which showed that of 12 measurable MDGs, Mozambique was unlikely to reach four: share of the poorest fifth in national consumption, child malnutrition, under-five mortality and children in upper primary education (6th and 7th grade). The report showed that despite continuing official GDP growth of more than 7% a year for nearly a decade, there has been a dramatic fall in real GDP per capita from $ 210 in 1998 to $ 131 in 2002, and that this had risen to only $ 149 in 2004 – the last year for which data were available. The report found that although the human development index was rising steadily, the percentage of underweight children and low birth-weight babies was improving only very slowly.

Donors are increasingly concerned about *corruption*. The April evaluation found that government had met 23 of 26 economic and development targets, but only 5 of 13 governance targets. In another British department for international development report, Tony Vaux in April warned that despite Mozambique's positive progress and willingness to engage with the agenda of donors, the trend was towards centralization and consolidation of power within a narrow elite, which will be obliged to offer patronage to a wide and 'greedy' circle of clients. The tendency towards corruption will undermine development and democratic processes, potentially creating a vicious spiral.

USAID issued a report in May that claimed "political considerations dominate the highest level of the *court system*", while justice officials "sell verdicts and lose evidence and case files in exchange for bribes." There is "active involvement of individuals within government or the ruling party in criminal activity, including drug trafficking, money laundering and theft of public funds." The report personally attacked supreme court President Mario Mangaze, who is given "a significant portion of the blame for slow reform" of the justice system. "He is a Frelimo stalwart who is widely considered to be a key interlocutor for political leaders when important interests are at stake in court cases."

Attorney-General Joaquim Madeira on 11 April told parliament that "chronic situations of manifest corruption" in the criminal investigation police, PIC ('Polícia de Investigação Criminal'), even involving high-ranking officers, "leave us in despair and suffocate the work of the honest." He said that some officers had blocked the investigation of the assassination of journalist Carlos Cardoso in 2000 and had been taken off the case, but were subsequently promoted. In his speech, he called for PIC to be transferred from the notoriously corrupt interior ministry to become part of a public prosecutors' office, but later in the year this was blocked politically.

Donors had forced the government to carry out a forensic audit of the plundered and collapsed *Austral* bank, and the audit was delivered early in the year. Although it was believed to highlight high-level corruption and might point to the killer in 2000 of the acting head of the bank, António Siba-Siba Macuacaua, no action had been taken on the report. After ten years during which it was managed by the British company, the Crown Agents, Mozambique took back control of its customs service on 5 July.

The *administrative tribunal*, TA ('Tribunal Administrativo', a kind of auditor-general), reported at the end of the year on the government's 2005 accounts. The report exposed some corruption and a lot of incompetence. It also highlighted loans to the elite, which are not being repaid. A highly controversial issue has been more than $ 40 m in loans made to companies by the state treasury in 1999 to 2002: many of these had been *political loans*, or at least reflected a conflict of interest. For example, a company partly owned by Albano Silva received a loan when his wife, Luisa Diogo, was finance minister. The TA reported that of 42 companies that received loans from the treasury, only 13 had made any repayments by the end of 2005. Silva's company is repaying its loan. A company partly owned by President Armando Guebuza has repaid only 1% of its loan, but companies linked to other members of the Frelimo elite are not repaying. Meanwhile, when Banco Austral collapsed and was renationalised and then re-privatised in 2002 (to ABSA in South Africa, itself taken over by Barclays), 70 loans for $ 17 m were left for the state to collect. These are believed to be the politically sensitive loans. By the end of 2005, only 15% had been collected. Of the 70 bad loans, attempts were being made to collect 44, while 26 "are still being analysed". The TA report also analysed income and expenditure and made some interesting points, for example, that twice as much is spent on each school pupil in Maputo city as in Zambezia. In health, the spending in Maputo city per person is three times the spending in Nampula province.

Labour Minister Helena Taipo took a hard line on employers not meeting proper *labour standards*, including those in cashew factories in the north of the country. But the most public conflict was with the British firm Group 4 Securicor and its subsidiary Wackenhut. An arbitration panel ruled in 2005 that Wackenhut had improperly failed to pay overtime since 1994 to 600 workers, and that it owed present and former workers $ 1.36 m. Wackenhut refused to pay, and on 28 August Taipo issued a formal order insisting on payment. Then the company lost the contract to guard the US embassy and in November dismissed 250 staff without compensation. The labour ministry ruled that the company owed the staff a total of $ 300,000 in redundancy pay. Local managing director

Jon Mortimer held a press conference at which he stated his refusal to pay. In December, Taipo withdrew his work permit.

Mozambique's press is now freer than that in the US, according to Reporters Without Borders in their annual *press freedom* index. In the ranking, Mozambique came 45th and the US 53rd. In 2002, the US was number 17 and Mozambique ranked 70th.

An *earthquake* on 23 February measuring 7.5 on the Richter scale was the strongest in recorded history in the country. It was centred in remote Machaze district and caused little damage. The earthquake was felt 530 km away in Maputo, where tall buildings swayed. The total lack of damage there is due to strict building codes, which took into account that Mozambique is in an earthquake zone. *Landmines* and unexploded ordinance from three wars continued to be a problem, with 23 people killed in 2005 compared to only three in 2004, Deputy Foreign Minister Henrique Banze said on 13 July.

On 1 July, the country switched over to a *new metical* (MTn), which simply drops three os off the old currency. Old coins and banknotes were slowly replaced: they were no longer legal tender in shops but could be exchanged in banks for several more years. On 2 May, the *minimum wage* was increased from the equivalent of $ 53 per month to $ 56.60: for agricultural workers the rise was from $ 38.10 to $ 40.15 per month.

Electrification expanded rapidly. The final provincial capital, Lichinga, was linked to the national grid on 17 April, and the grid should reach all 128 district capitals by 2010. The government has stepped up development of bio-fuels based on agricultural products: work started on two factories. Wherever he went, President Guebuza urged peasants to grow jatropha. Previously treated as a weed, its seeds can be pressed locally for an oil that can be used in lamps, and when pressed commercially can be mixed with diesel.

The grain harvest was 2.1 m tonnes, up 10% on 2005. Pulse and cassava production were also up. On 16 January, Industry and Trade Minister Antonio Fernando launched a *Made in Mozambique* campaign to encourage people to buy locally made goods.

Mozambique in 2007

Mozambique remains the donor darling, with aid rising. The economy continues to grow at more than 7% a year, but a series of reports pointed to increasing inequality and noted that growth is not reaching the poor. Floods and other disasters made their mark. Provincial elections were postponed.

Domestic Politics

Elections dominated the political scene. There should have been provincial assembly elections in 2007, followed by local elections in 2008 and national elections (for parliament and president) in 2009. However, parliament was very slow in enacting legislation and only approved new electoral legislation in different stages during March. Parliament appointed its members of the *National Election Commission* (CNE) only in May, with three members from the governing Frelimo party and two from the Renamo opposition. In June, these five selected eight further members from 62 candidates proposed by civil society organisations. The civil society members are all seen as being close to Frelimo. By law, the CNE president must be one of the civil society members and the CNE selected João Leopoldo da Costa, rector of the private university ISCTEM. The CNE serves for five years.

A revised constitution created assemblies in the 10 provinces, and they were to be elected before 19 January 2008. The date for *provincial elections* was first set for 20 December, then moved to 16 January 2008 at the height of the rainy season and finally parliament passed a constitutional amendment allowing them to take place at the same time as national elections in 2009. The electoral

 | DOI 10.1163/9789004301122_005

law required a completely new *registration* and with the very late appointment of the CNE it proved impossible to undertake this exercise in time. Registration was also extended several times, and by early 2008 more than eight million of 10 million voting age adults had registered.

International observers had severely criticised what they saw as a unique *secret vote tabulation* process, which in 2004 allowed the CNE to exclude the results of more than 5% of polling stations and change the results of others without explanation. An analysis of the election results by the London School of Economics Crisis States Programme, released in 2007, found "that ballot box stuffing, improper ballot nullification, and (intentional) organisational failure took place". Mozambique's own constitutional council criticised the lack of transparency and said the CNE had acted improperly. The new CNE has also been accused of impropriety by the local press, because it ignored the clause in the *electoral law* which stated that CNE members cannot have other paid employment, yet most civil society nominees retained their old posts. Parliament did not modify the parts of the legislation allowing for secrecy and the new CNE refused to even consider more openness. At a 27 June meeting with Foreign Minister Alcinda Abreu, donors flatly refused to fund the election without assurances of transparency and international observation. The European Commission had already set up a budget line to fund the election, but withdrew the offer. Ironically, the fall in the value of the dollar against the euro and pound meant that budget support increased by enough in dollars to pay for the election and registration. However, the issue remained unresolved.

On other issues, there was a big push towards decentralisation, built around district planning. In 2007, each of the 128 districts was given Metical 7 m (about $ 240,000) for economic development and job creation. *Local consultative councils* were set up in each district and at three lower tiers – administrative post, locality and village. The consultative councils were nominated rather than elected but must be broadly representative. They have a strong voice in the spending of the Metical 7 m and in local development plans, and thus brought at least 50,000 people into the decision-making process. The councils were also expected to monitor repayment of loans from the Metical 7 m, comment on projects by non-government organisations in their area and have a say on land and natural resource concessions. The move has involved a surprising degree of experimentation. Initially, the money was given to each district with virtually no instructions, and central government watched how it was used and how communities responded. New rules were issued, often in confusingly close succession, to stop money from being spent on administrators' cars and offices and then to direct it towards economic goals and job creation. Councils were restructured to ensure they had more women and were more representative.

The *agriculture ministry* suffered a series of traumas. Minister Tomas Mandlate was dismissed on 23 February and replaced by Erasmo Muhate. A fire destroyed a third of the ministry on 25 May, including important historic records, and pointed to the lack of fire fighting capacity. On 10 December, Muhate was sacked after he dismissed eight of his directors and deputy directors. Soares Nhaca, a former trade union leader and governor, was named to replace him.

President Armando Guebuza named Filipe Couto rector of Universidade Eduardo Mondlane, the country's oldest and largest university, against the advice of the university council. A Catholic priest who built the Catholic University, he is the brother of deputy finance minister Pedro Couto.

The Christian Council reported that in the 25 years since the end of the civil war, it has collected 700,000 guns as part of its programme to trade guns for hoes.

Foreign Affairs

Foreign affairs meant donor relations and Mozambique remained a *donor darling*. An IMF review on 2 February said: "Mozambique is a success story in Sub-Saharan Africa, benefiting from sustained large foreign aid inflows, strong and broad-based growth and deep poverty reduction". Aid continued to rise, from $ 1,228 m in 2004 to $ 1,273 in 2005 and $ 1,473 in 2006 (all excluding debt cancellation, which officially counts as 'aid'). Aid was one-fifth GDP and half of the government budget. Mozambique received 70% more aid per capita than its neighbours Tanzania and Malawi ($ 74 per capita compared to $ 44 for the other two). The largest donor is the EU ($ 174 m) followed by the US, UK and Sweden.

Nineteen donors (all the major donors except the US and Japan) are part of the *budget support group*, which now is also the major forum for policy discussion with the government. One-quarter of all aid (excluding debt cancellation) goes directly into the government budget and the donors in 2007 pledged a 10% increase in budget support for 2008, to $ 435 m. Nevertheless, there is growing disquiet. A joint *aide memoir*, agreed on 21 September, praised the government's macroeconomic successes, but threatened cuts if the government failed to act on corruption, governance and the courts. Such threats had been made in the past, but Denmark became the first country to reduce budget support (by 17%) and Germany's pledge for 2008, although still an increase, was smaller than originally announced. After two years of delay, the US Millennium Challenge Corporation on 13 July finally signed an agreement for $ 507 m for water, sanitation and roads in the north of Mozambique.

The *Cahora Bassa dam* finally reverted to the Mozambican government on 27 November, two years after the Portuguese government first agreed to sell it. Mozambique paid $ 700 m, borrowed from a consortium of banks, to Portugal for 67% of the dam. Mozambique now owns 85% and Portugal 15%. Portugal was anxious to make the deal because it needed the money to reduce its own deficit to meet EU criteria.

Mozambique's relations with its neighbours continued to be good, but the crisis in *Zimbabwe* continued to have an impact, reducing traffic through the ports and driving Zimbabweans over the border to look for work in Mozambique. Officially, Mozambique backed SADC attempts to press President Robert Mugabe to stand down. As soon as it took over the Cahora Bassa dam, government stepped up the pressure. Zimbabwe had a debt of $ 19 m for electricity from the dam, so supplies were halved in mid-December and then cut off on 28 December. Zimbabwe paid half of its debt, and some power was restored.

Former President *Joaquim Chissano* won $ 5 m over ten years and then $ 200,000 a year for life in the inaugural round of a prize sponsored by the private telecom business tycoon Mo Ibrahim. The citations mentioned his achievements in bringing peace and reconciliation after the war. The prize was only given to a president who had voluntarily stepped down in the previous three years. The citation carefully did not mention governance or corruption. Chissano did not stand in 2004 because the Frelimo party did not select him as a candidate, fearing that he would lose because the reputation of those close to him for corruption was too strong. Chissano's son Nyimpine died during the year. He had been charged with ordering the murder of Mozambique's most important journalist, Carlos Cardoso, in 2000. Chissano also served as a special envoy to the secretary general of the UN during the year, including missions to Uganda and Sudan.

Socioeconomic Developments

A string of disasters hit Mozambique. *Floods* in the Zambezi River valley in February and March were the worst since 2002 and displaced 110,000 people. A further 175,000 lost crops or saw their homes damaged. Efforts were made to encourage people to move out of high risk areas, but most people returned to their old land and ran the risk of being dislodged again. Mozambique's disaster relief agency is now well managed and maintained effective control throughout both floods. Help came from the World Food Programme and a small group of international non-government agencies (INGOs) that have a long working relationship with the government. No emergency appeal was issued for the flood, despite pressure from INGOs, which wanted to use it for fund-raising and fed exaggerated stories to the BBC and other press. One of Mozambique's biggest problems was fending off agencies who sent teams to Mozambique to 'help', but who mostly caused problems.

An unusually strong cyclone, Favio, with winds of up to 180 kph, made a direct hit on the tourist city of Vilankulu on 22 February, causing major damage. Not surprisingly, *climate change* has become a prominent issue. In late March, there was unprecedented flooding of low-lying coastal areas. Although this happened during a sun-moon-earth alignment that caused very high tides, it may also have been a mark of rising sea levels. Reports by various agencies released during the year gave mixed forecasts, but all seemed to agree that the south of Mozambique was going to become even drier, putting an end to rain-fed agriculture. Speaking at the UN General Assembly on 26 September, President Guebuza said Mozambique was already feeling the impact of climate change, and he called on the rich countries to take action to reduce emissions.

On 22 March, an *explosion at a military arsenal* in the capital city of Maputo killed 103 people, injured 515 and destroyed or damaged more than 1,300 houses. The arsenal housed obsolete Portuguese weapons dating back to the colonial era and Soviet munitions from the war of destabilisation. At least 4,000 shells and rockets were hurled out by the explosion and Soviet rockets were found more than 10 kilometres away. After an explosion at the arsenal in 1985 killed 13 people, it was recommended that it be closed, but nothing was done. After a similar explosion at a Beira arsenal in 2002, Russia offered equipment and technicians to disarm and dismantle the weapons, but the offer was not taken up.

A *national census* showed a population of 20,530,714, up 28% on the 1997 population of 16,075,708. The capital Maputo now had 1,100,000 people. Matola, which adjoins Maputo, is now the second largest city, with 675,000. This means that capital zone, including suburbs, has more than two million people. Nampula is now the third largest city with 478,000 people, while Beira fell back to fourth position with 436,000. Next came Chimoio 239,000, Nacala 207,000 and Quelimane 192,000.

A detailed survey during the year revealed that there are 162,424 *civil servants*, including teachers and health workers. This first-ever survey was done by teams from the civil service commission, which went to district capitals to register each civil servant. The system used computers, and it is a mark of the underdevelopment of Mozambique that 50 of 128 districts did not have stable electricity and adequate telecommunications for the computers to be used. In these instances, civil servants had to go to the nearest district with electricity and telephone to register.

Although malaria is still the biggest killer, *HIV/AIDS* is a growing problem. By the end of the year, nearly 100,000 people were receiving antiretroviral (ARV) drugs. This is still only one-third of those who could benefit from them, and many of those using ARVs are so poor they cannot afford adequate food.

Supreme Court President Mario Mangaze reported an improvement in *prisons*. Previously, most people held in Mozambican jails had been found guilty of nothing, but were simply awaiting trial. That had been reversed. By year's end, 66% of the prison population consisted of people serving sentences, while only 34% were on remand.

The national electricity grid continued to be expanded, and by the end of 2007 had reached 70 of 128 district capitals. A study by the ministry of planning and development noted that within just a few years Mozambique will become "a highly *resource dependent economy* comparable to countries like the Republic of Congo, Gabon, Norway, Trinidad and Tobago, and Zambia." Mozambique is committed to "follow the principles" of the Extractive Industries Transparency Initiative (EITI), but there is growing concern both in the international community and civil society about the lack of transparency with respect to resource revenues. Mozambique already exports electricity and uses it to smelt aluminium. Plans are far advanced for a second dam, Mphanda Nkuwa, on the Zambezi. Prime Minister Luisa Diogo reported in November that investors were being sought for gas and coal-fired power stations as well. Gas is exported to South Africa and exploration reports indicated further gas fields off the coast of central Mozambique. President Armando Guebuza visited US oil companies in Texas in September and was told that there are probably exploitable quantities of oil in the north. Two major coal-mining projects are also under way, mainly to export coking coal for steel production to Brazil and India. The first titanium mine, owned by the Irish company Kenmare, began production in October and a second mine is planned. It is expected that Mozambique's exports will shortly be 40% aluminium, 40% minerals and energy and just 20% agricultural and other goods.

With the rapidly rising price of oil, production of *biofuel* for local consumption and export became more interesting. For several years, President Armando Guebuza has promoted jatropha, which can be grown on marginal grounds, and several small companies planned to start refining oil for oilseeds into biodiesel. In December, work began on the largest project, a sugar plantation dedicated entirely to the production of 480,000 litres per day of ethanol to add to petrol. The project is controversial, because it uses water from the Massingir dam, which, it was argued, would be better used to produce rice. The debate continued throughout the year. The government rejected other proposals from foreign investors to use large tracts of land for biofuels, and government ministers stressed fuel production should not compete with food.

Despite President Guebuza's repeatedly calling for a 'green revolution', for example at a Frelimo central committee meeting on 15 March, *agricultural development* remained very limited, with little research or investment. However, there has been interest in three traditional sectors. Tongaat-Hulett in January announced plans to spend $ 180 m on expanding their sugar plantations. Cashew production has been slowly recovering after the government reversed World Bank-imposed policies and began to support the sector. Producers marketed 76,000 tonnes of cashew in the 2005–06 season, up from 63,000 tonnes the previous season. About half of the crop was used by Mozambican processing factories and half exported to India for processing. Peasant cotton production for the 2005–06 season was the highest in 35 years.

Tobacco has become Mozambique's third most important export, after aluminium and electricity, and is more important than gas, prawns or sugar. Exports in 2006 were $ 110 m, fives time the level of just four years earlier. About 150,000 peasant families produced tobacco. Only half made a profit but the one-quarter who were the most successful growers averaged $ 900 a year of profit. Tobacco has been the only crop to raise peasant incomes and the only crop to increase fertiliser use – tobacco farmers were ten times more likely to use fertiliser on maize than those who do not also grow tobacco. Tobacco is run on a concession system, like cotton. A company is given exclusive rights to a district and provides credit and extension services to peasants in the district, who must sell their tobacco to that company. Tobacco depends on exploitation of family labour, so that tobacco farmers are less likely to send their children to school. Meanwhile, new laws came into force banning smoking in restaurants and many other public places. On 29 May, the government increased the minimum wage from the equivalent of $ 40 a month to $ 44 for agricultural workers and from $ 56 per month to $ 64 for other workers.

A report on *illegal logging* was followed up by press reports that painted a picture of incompetence and corruption that has allowed traders to strip Mozambican forests of valuable hardwoods and ship them to Asia. During the year, containers of illegal logs were seized in the ports of Pemba and Nacala.

GDP growth continued at over 7%, although inflation was 12.1%, nearly double the target of 6.4%. Food and fuel prices rose and the urban poor became poorer. Although the World Bank and IMF praised Mozambique's rapid growth, Paulo Cuinica, secretary general of the G20 NGO platform, said that on the ground people did not feel the economic growth. When President Guebuza toured the country, he faced increasing complaints about crime and of corrupt police who did nothing. As the year progressed, tensions increased in poor neighbourhoods of big cities and at least a dozen young men accused of crimes were lynched – in Maputo they used the South African technique of 'necklacing' in which a tyre is put over the victim's head, filled with petrol and set alight.

Three studies released early in the year pointed to growing differentiation and *increasing poverty.* Two studies compared rural income surveys in 1995–96, 2001–02 and 2004–05. Officially, 70% of the population was rural, so this also included people in smaller towns. There was a general increase in income between the first two surveys, but of the total increase in rural income 73% went to the fifth of households with the highest incomes and less than 3% went to the poorest fifth. For the next period, 2001–02 to 2004–05, differentiation accelerated. The poorest half of the rural population actually saw their incomes fall, while the top fifth made another large gain. Finally, the studies showed that the position of people near the poverty line was very precarious. Half of the rural families considered 'not poor' in 2001–02 had fallen back into poverty by 2004–05.

The other study, "Beating the Odds" by the World Bank, noted "the blistering pace of economic growth" but went on to say that "rural income inequality seems to be growing, and already high urban inequality persists, so that the same high growth has less of a poverty reducing effect". It added: "Continued growth after 2003 has not been trickling down to the poor". Indeed, increasing costs of living seemed to hit the poorest hardest, the report noted. A key marker is "how little children's nutritional status has changed" – economic growth was not increasing food consumption by the poor, and the poor were also less likely to use health services and send their children to school. Various studies showed that jobs were an important way to escape poverty, but in rural areas most people were too poor to hire labour. The World Bank study also noted that Mozambique had suffered from *job destruction*, shedding jobs at more than 10% a year on average as part of privatisation and restructuring. The 'mega-projects' such as aluminium and gas have created a few jobs, but not enough to compensate – so despite the rapid GDP growth, there were fewer jobs.

'*Lazy peasants*' became an issue in April. Speaking at a rally in Zambezia province, President Guebuza said, "the lack of habit of hard work is perpetuating hunger and poverty. There are too many lazybones in Mozambique. We have to admit we don't work much". This brought an angry response from the National Peasants Association, which called on government to provide agricultural credit and the fertiliser and improved seeds that peasants were too poor to buy. Just days later, the national food security unit reported that *chronic malnutrition* among children was increasing. Clearly peasants were too poor to feed their children properly and did not have enough food to work hard in their fields.

A report issued by the UNDP International Poverty Centre in Brasilia in September said Mozambique's development strategy was not pro-poor and required a "significant shift". Investment in agriculture was "extremely low" and productivity had not changed in the past decade. There was a big rise in inequality, with growth going only to consumption by the richest. The stress on the big mineral-energy projects has led to the loss of more jobs than have been created, and the "overall impact has arguably been to increase poverty". Government, it said, had "*no overarching development vision*".

Mozambique in 2008

Frelimo's sweeping victory in local elections cemented its position as the predominant party. Renamo became increasingly insignifi cant. A cabinet reshuffle showed no fundamental political changes. The corruption crackdown netted some high profile arrests. Xenophobia in South Africa and the crisis in Zimbabwe were the most important subregional external factors impacting on foreign relations, while the negotiations with donors remained essential both in foreign affairs as well as socioeconomic developments. Economic growth continued, but worsening poverty triggered sporadic violence.

Domestic Politics

The ruling Frelimo party overwhelmed an ever-weaker opposition in *local elections* on 19 November, winning a majority in the municipal assembly and mayoral office in 42 of 43 municipalities. Renamo, the former guerrilla movement and now the main opposition, had won control of five of the then 33 municipalities in 2003, but lost them all. Blame was largely laid at the door of Renamo President Afonso Dhlakama, and Renamo was expected to do badly in national elections due in late 2009. Frelimo was the single liberation movement that won independence in 1975, then ruled the one party state, and has won all multi-party elections since the end of the civil war in 1992. It has always had an extensive and responsive party structure reaching down to the smallest village, and under President Armando Guebuza this was strengthened and revitalised. Indeed, there were growing complaints that civil servants and those applying for government loans

 | DOI 10.1163/9789004301122_006

and licences were now expected to have party cards. The party machine has become increasingly effective in two ways. First, it transmits grassroots concerns to the top, as has been shown by Guebuza's increasing emphasis on job creation, which is a major local preoccupation. Second, it has been highly effective in encouraging its supporters to vote. Turnout in the local elections was 46%, compared to 28% in the 2003 municipal elections and 43% in the 2004 national elections. By contrast, Dhlakama, who has led Renamo since it was a South African-backed guerrilla movement in the 1980s, has retained tightly centralised control and has failed to convert Renamo into an effective political party. Fearing challenges to his leadership, he expelled or marginalised people with political and organising skills. The reason for the devastating defeat in local elections was largely due to the lack of a party machine to support local candidates and mobilise sympathisers and ensure they voted.

Beira, Mozambique's third largest city, could prove to be Dhlakama's downfall. Since colonial times, Beira has always opposed the government in the capital and it has become a Renamo stronghold. Daviz Simango was elected mayor in 2003 and proved to be highly effective and popular and it was assumed he would stand again for re-election. Just days before candidates' lists were to be submitted, Dhlakama announced that the unpopular Renamo party head in the province, Manuel Pereira, would be the candidate. Simango supporters were outraged and in three days organised enough signatures to allow him to stand as an independent. Simango won 62% of the vote, compared to 34% for the Frelimo candidate and a derisory 3% for Pereira. Dhlakama expelled Simango from the party, but many in Renamo, especially younger activists but also parliamentary leaders, support Simango as the person with the charisma and organising skills to revitalise the party. At the end of the year, Dhlakama was tenaciously retaining control of a party in increasing disarray.

The next test will be *national elections* in 2009 – for president, national parliament and, for the first time, for new provincial parliaments. Provincial parliaments were included in the 2002 constitution at the insistence of Dhlakama, who believed Renamo would win majorities in at least half the provinces – a now highly dubious assumption. Provincial elections had been scheduled for 2007, but were postponed to correspond with national elections in 2009. A new electoral register was drawn up during three registration periods in 2007 and 2008. More than 8.9 m people registered to vote, 88% of the voting age population of 10.2 m. Mozambique has two local government systems: in rural areas district administrators are appointed by central government, but urban areas are municipalities with elected governments and substantial devolved powers, including for economic development. The number of municipalities was increased from 33 to 43 and they cover 31% of the national population.

Meanwhile, Frelimo is combining moves to both *centralise and decentralise*, with an understanding that these are not incompatible. Party membership and obedience to both government policy and party leaders are increasingly demanded, with instructions often passed down the line by mobile telephone, but within that system power has been substantially decentralised and creativity is encouraged in the carrying out of policy. The mayor of Maputo, Eneas Comiche, had proved to be highly effective, but Frelimo did not choose him to stand again because he was seen as too independent of party leadership. Unlike Renamo, the decision caused some local anger but no defections. The new Maputo mayor is David Simango. The two Simangos are unrelated, but the two big city mayors with names that differ by only one letter caused immense confusion in the foreign media and donor communities.

The biggest example of centralisation mixed with decentralisation is the *district development fund* created by the Guebuza government. More than $ 300,000 per year is given to each district and rules were tightened in 2008 so that money could only go for projects that create jobs or increase food production, and that can repay the loan. Decisions are made by local district and village development committees, which must have at least 30% women and be genuinely representative of local interest groups. Informally, most members are Frelimo. But within those rules, the local development committees have almost total discretion to decide on loans and monitor the projects, which means for the first time literally tens of thousands of people are making decisions about how development money is to be spent. The funds also show the degree of communication between top and bottom. Initially, some of the money could be spent on small infrastructure, but central government decided this was already in the state budget and should not be allowed. Development committees objected, saying they wanted the ability to commission locally essential small projects such as drainage, bridges and classrooms that were not in provincial and national plans, and in 2008 this was agreed and a second grant of $ 100,000 per district was given for locally determined infrastructure. In addition to these grants, communities earned $ 1.4 m in 2007 from local management of forestry, wildlife and other resources, up more than 50% from 2006. Permanent secretary in the agriculture ministry, Daniel Clemente, said that 68 community management projects were being implemented, 70% being supervised by foreign donors and the remainder by national organisations.

A *government reshuffle*, which began in December 2007 with the sacking of the agriculture minister and the appointment of former trade union leader and former provincial governor Soares Nhaca as his replacement continued in March. The defence, foreign affairs, justice, transport and environment ministers, all considered weak, were sacked. Oldemiro Baloi, a respected former industry minister and deputy cooperation minister who had become a banker, was named foreign minister. The new justice minister, Benvinda Levy, is a judge; the new transport minister Paulo Zucula had won praise as head of the National Disasters Institute (INGC). Frelimo political commission member Alcinda Abreu was demoted from foreign affairs to environment minister. Dismissed defence minister Tobias Dai is President Armando Guebuza's brother-in-law. Filipe Nhussi, a former businessman, is the first defence minister not to have been in the liberation war, but the link is retained because he is a Makonde from the north of the country and his parents fought in the liberation war. The army's chief of staff and deputy chief of staff, who had held the posts since the end of the war 14 years ago, finally retired in March. Like their predecessors, the new chief of staff is Frelimo and the deputy is Renamo and all four were commanders in the 1982–92 war.

Corruption remained a central issue, both with government and donors. Budget support was not increased and money going to projects and programmes was not being converted into budget support, due to "serious disquiet about performance in the area of governance, particularly the lack of substantive indications of progress in the fight against corruption," said Irish ambassador Frank Sheridan, head of the G19 donor budget support group, on 22 May. "Concerns about governance have been growing in recent years, and could have a long term influence if we do not find ways together of making tangible progress," he added. A touchstone for donors has been the failure to bring prosecutions over the looting of Banco Austral by people high in Frelimo in the late 1990s and the assassination in 2001 of Bank of Mozambique head of banking supervision Antonio Siba-Siba Macuacua, who had introduced a vigorous loan recovery programme. Under donor pressure, the government ordered a forensic audit of Austral by an international law firm. Although that audit was completed in 2006, nothing has happened. The results of the audit have not been made public and nobody has been arrested for fraud or malfeasance. "The lack of progress in criminal investigations following up the forensic audit of Banco Austral remains a recurrent preoccupation of the partners," said the Norwegian ambassador and 2007–08 G19 head, Thorbjørn Gaustadsaether, on 30 April.

Corruption was also of concern to Mozambicans, and after a relative silence in the first half of the year the government announced a whole series of *corruption-related actions*. On 22 September, Almerino Manhenje, who had been interior minister from 1996 to 2005 and who was seen as close to former President Joaquim Chissano, was arrested and charged with involvement in the case of $ 9 m missing from the interior ministry. He was not granted bail and remained in detention in early 2009. Eight others were also arrested, including the financial directors of the interior ministry and the riot police. Arrested separately on 22 September was Albino Mussana, former director of the national social security institute. He had been dismissed in February and in June Labour Minister Helena Taipo said that $ 8 m had been stolen from the social security fund between 2002 and 2008. Former Transport Minister Antonio Munguambe and Diodino Cambaze, head of the Mozambique Airports Company, were arrested in December and October respectively and charged with corruption relating to airport company funds. A former administrator of Banco Austral, Benigno Parent Junior, and two security guards were arrested on 8 December and charged with the murder of Antonio Siba-Siba Macuacua. Three senior officials of the bank at that time had been interviewed by the police in July. Despite *prima facie* evidence of the violation of banking and company laws, no one has been charged with plundering the bank and senior Frelimo officials suspected of involvement still retain high level protection. Government spokesman and Deputy Education Minister Luis Covane reported that 468 public servants were dismissed or expelled from the state apparatus, compared to 461 in 2007. These sanctions were imposed for such offences as theft of state funds, forgery of documents and signatures, breaches of professional secrecy, absence from work without authorisation, poor attendance to the public and drunkenness at work. The 'Universidade Pedagogica' (teacher training university) expelled 238 students for falsifying the certificates that showed they had completed the 12th class of secondary school. Two Pakistani citizens were caught trying to smuggle over $ 2.5 m in bank notes out of Mozambique. They were stopped by the customs service at Machipanda, on the border with Zimbabwe.

However, *high-level corruption* remained an issue. On 7 December, three notorious murderers were allowed to escape from cells in the Maputo city police command. They were Anibal dos Santos Junior ('Anibalzinho'), the man who led the death squad that murdered the country's foremost investigative journalist, Carlos Cardoso, in November 2000. He has twice before been allowed to escape by high interior ministry officials. Escaping with Anibalzinho were Custodio Luis de Jesus ('Todinho'), charged with the murder of the director of the Maputo central prison, and Samuel Chavangueza ('Samito'), accused of a string of bank robberies and murders of police officers. They were alleged to be closely linked to police and interior ministry staff who were directly involved in organised crime, and those who released them may have been anxious to prevent them testifying in upcoming court cases. Todinho was shot and killed in Maputo in mid-January 2009 in very unclear circumstances, while Samito was arrested again. A fire was set in a building of the finance ministry on

22 October, according to the deputy prosecutor, Taibo Mucobora. The building housed the budget and accounts sections. The fire was extinguished relatively quickly and did not damage any key documents.

An article in the government daily 'Noticias' (16 October) claimed that police who had stopped *overweight vehicles* on the toll road from Maputo to South Africa received mobile telephone calls from 'influential individuals' telling them to release the lorry. Drivers simply used their mobile phone to contact these 'influential individuals' if they were stopped. The problem was so common that it made controlling heavy vehicles very difficult. More than one-third of lorries weighed during the year had been overweight, according to the company that runs the toll road.

Foreign Affairs

Mozambique was one of the first countries to participate in the APRM. It prepared its self-appraisal and the first AU team visited. The xenophobic violence that erupted in May in *South Africa* dominated foreign affairs. At least 30 Mozambicans were killed and 37,000 Mozambicans fled. The other major issue was the crisis in *Zimbabwe* and the question of how to deal with President Robert Mugabe. This had a direct effect on Mozambique, with many impoverished Zimbabweans crossing the border into Mozambique in search of work and a sharp drop in traffic passing through the port of Beira. Despite this, most of Mozambique's leadership tended to support Mugabe, both because they feel a debt for Mugabe's support during the destabilisation war in the 1980s and because they feared that if Mugabe fell, donors would force the reversal of land reform. But Graça Machel, widow of first President Samora Machel and wife of South Africa's former

President Nelson Mandela, called for increased regional pressure on Mugabe to step down. When the Cahora Bassa dam passed into Mozambican ownership, the new management immediately cut electricity supplies to Zimbabwe until some of the large back debt was paid 12 days later.

Donor relations remained largely good, despite concerns about the failure to deal with corruption. But in a 30 April report, donors admitted that they were failing to keep their promises and failing to reduce the workload for the government. For example, the budget support donors sent 191 missions to Mozambique in 2007 – meaning one arrived nearly every working day – and totally failed to keep their pledge to reduce missions to 140. They also failed to cooperate more on technical assistance. In an unusually angry comment, Mozambique's Planning and Development Minister Aiuba Cuereneia on 30 April said, "we must mention, as we have in every joint review, the need to reduce the administrative burden of foreign aid, including the duration of joint and semi-annual reviews, which continue to be very long and complex, absorbing too much work time of senior members of the government and partners."

Foreign aid remained essential. Finance Minister Manuel Chang said aid would cover 56% of government expenditure. Roughly half of aid is direct budget support. The policy dialogue with government has been dominated by the group of 19 donors. They gave money directly to the state budget, in part because they collectively negotiated conditionality with the government and the size of budget support gave them huge power. The World Bank was a member of the G19. The US and Japan wanted to maintain tighter detailed control over how their aid was dispersed and refused to give aid as budget support. As major donors, they objected to having so little influence and being excluded from the policy dialogue. Thus, towards the end of the year, there were informal discussions about how to create a joint policy forum. After four years of negotiations, the US finally began to dispense funds from a $ 507 m Millennium Challenge Account grant.

Both Sweden and Switzerland reduced their budget support, as the World Bank and Denmark had done a year before. In an action that won public praise from both critics and supporters, the government finally *stood up to the donors* in mid-August, when President Armando Guebuza and Development Minister Aiuba Cuereneia said that government would use its own revenues to fill the gap.

Socioeconomic Developments

Economic growth was estimated at 6.8%, not far short of the target of 7%, Prime Minister Luisa Diogo said on 27 December. The capital Maputo displayed major new construction and traffic jams of new cars. However, there was growing recognition that the majority of Mozambicans were not benefiting from economic growth. The joint AfDB, OECD and ECA report “African Economic Outlook” warned that growth was largely driven by aid and by “mega-projects” such as the Mozal aluminium smelter, which generated little in terms of employment or tax revenue. “Although the tendency for poverty reduction continues, there are also perceptions and clear indications of an ever growing *gulf between the privileged and the poorest*”, Norwegian ambassador Thorbjørn Gaustadsaether said at the closing ceremony of the joint review on 30 April. He added that various factors, notably the lack of jobs, meant that “the least favoured members of society have not benefited from the country’s economic growth.” The 2008–9 G19 chair, Irish ambassador Frank Sheridan, said “it seems to me that many of the poorest are struggling just to maintain their present standard of living, or are even falling back, while the most prosperous are benefiting disproportionately." He warned that failure to deal with problems of inequality could lead to "social tension and subsequent political failure", and thus he wanted to see "greater stress on economic growth that benefits the poorest." Even the IMF agreed. Age Bakker, head of an IMF mission to Mozambique, in a press conference at the end of February said that "most people do not feel the economic growth that has been registered in Mozambique. There must be more emphasis on an equitable distribution of wealth in the country." Bakker stressed the need to create jobs and to expand the financial sector to support agriculture.

Child *malnutrition* is rising, according to former Health Minister Helder Martins. Under-five malnutrition has risen from 36% in 1997 to 46% in 2006, he said on 19 June. Meanwhile, the government admitted it will not meet the MDGs for reducing *maternal and child mortality* rates. The rates were improving, but only slowly, according to National Director of Health Mouzinho Saide. For every 1,000 live births, 4 mothers die and 125 babies do not reach their fifth birthday, which remained extremely high. *Cholera* is now endemic in most of Mozambique and between October 2007 and the end of 2008 there were 15,000 cases and 170 deaths, a credibly low mortality rate of 1.1%, which reflects rapid response by health workers. More than 130,000 HIV-positive people were receiving anti-retroviral (ARV) drugs by the end of 2008, which is close to meeting the demand. The problem remained that many more people than that could benefit but refused to be tested, according to Health Minister Ivo Garrido.

Sporadic *violence* in response to growing poverty was an increasing issue. In demonstrations in Maputo on 5 February and four other towns on subsequent days against the high cost of living, at least five people were killed and more than 100 injured, many shot by the police. The demonstrations were typically organised by mobile telephone text message by young people, many in the 'informal sector', who built barriers and blocked the roads. Rogerio Sitoe, editor-in-chief of the government-owned daily 'Noticias' responded on 15 February in a remarkable column. He argued that the root cause of the riots was "the religious way we applaud and accept the prescriptions of the World Bank and International Monetary Fund," when these were really "poison prescriptions". They destroyed jobs and failed to promote agricultural development, which had "contributed greatly to the impoverishment of the countryside and forced a migration to the cities, particularly of the youth." The government needed instead its own development policy and to stop treating World Bank and IMF statements as if they were "bible verses".

Lynchings increased, with more than 50 people accused of being thieves being killed by communities during the year, and a similar number only saved by the police. The lynchings tend to be in very poor urban neighbourhoods, of people accused of stealing food from gardens or of breaking into houses at night in areas with no light or police protection. In poor rural areas in central Mozambique, several people were attacked and at least one killed when better-off farmers were accused of stealing the rain from their neighbours. In Cabo Delgado district in the north, local people burned down tents set up as cholera treatment units and attacked treatment teams, accusing them of spreading the disease. An earlier study by Carlos Serra and a team from Universidade Eduardo Mondlane of attacks on cholera teams showed the poor people believed strongly that the rich and powerful wanted to kill them and thus they could not accept that teams putting chlorine in wells were acting for their benefit.

Floods in January and February displaced more than 100,000 people in central Mozambique, mainly in the Zambezi river valley but also along the Save, Buzi and Pungoe rivers. At least 20 people died. In late January the Zambezi river at Tete rose by three metres in just two days. Flooding is a regular occurrence, and Mozambican preparations continue to improve, through the INGC. In September 2007, the regional meteorological forum SARCOF had predicted above average rainfall, so the INGC stepped up preparations. Evacuation committees were established in riverside villages and INGC organised boats and helicopters. As flooding became worse, it moved its headquarters to Caia on the Zambezi river to be closer to the action. INGC works with several aid agencies permanently based in Mozambique and they can increase their assistance during floods, but no special emergency appeal was issued. In mid-January, INGC head Paulo Zucula (appointed transport minister later in the year) held a press conference to criticise "organisations which live off of emergencies" and which were exaggerating the flood in order to raise money. On 18 February, all the Oxfams working collectively in Mozambique publicly apologised for a 4 January statement in which they claimed Mozambique had made a formal appeal for help.

In South Africa, 416 Mozambican *miners* died in 2007, according to figures released in 2008. Thirty-five died in accidents in the mines and the rest from other causes, mainly AIDS. In 2007, South African mines had recruited 45,000 Mozambicans, who remitted $ 93 m to Mozambique in 2008. In the six years 2002–07, 2,917 Mozambican miners had died and another 769 who were gravely ill were repatriated. New *minimum wages* were announced on 5 May. Previously there had been three minimum wages: $ 46 per month for agricultural workers, $ 59 for soldiers and $ 67 for other workers. The rates for other workers have now been split into nine categories, and the new minimum wages were: agricultural $ 54, soldiers $ 65, and others $ 75 to $ 97.

South Africa's electric power crisis affected Mozambique. In the first half of the year, the Mozal aluminium smelter (which imports electricity from South Africa rather than directly from Mozambique's Cahora Bassa dam) had to cut production by 10%. Two *biofuel* projects, both producing ethanol from sugar cane, were started during the period of high oil prices. One was in Dombe, Manica province, and will involve 18,000 hectares of sugar cane. The other is a $ 510 m project in Massingir district, Gaza province, with 30,000 hectares of sugar cane, to produce 120 m litres of ethanol a year. But this project is dependent on water from the Massingir dam, and a floodgate was seriously damaged on 22 May. The dam was built at the end of the colonial era and has never functioned properly. The central Mozambique *railway* line linking Tete coal mines and Zambezi valley sugar mills to the port of Beira was destroyed by Renamo in the mid-1980s during the war of destabilisation, but it is now being rebuilt. The line to the Marromeu sugar mill opened in 2008 and the line to Tete is due to open in 2010. Macao-based billionaire Stanley Ho has set up a bank, MozaBanco, chaired by former Bank of Mozambique governor Prakash Ratlal.

Cashew production hit 95,000 tonnes in the 2007–08 harvest, above the target of 85,000 tonnes. Of this, about one third was exported raw, mainly to India, one third was processed by the rapidly expanding group of local factories and the remaining third was processed by the informal sector. The average export prices for unprocessed nuts was $ 750 per tonne, up more than 50% on 2007, according to the director of the government's Cashew Promotion Institute (INCAJU), Filomena Maiopue. This, in turn, pushed up the price paid to peasants to over $ 0.5 per kg. The revival of the cashew sector started in 2001 when Mozambique quietly rejected the World Bank-imposed free market policy, which had destroyed the sector, and instead began supporting peasant producers, marketing associations and private factories.

Mozambique's *foreign debt* is $ 3.3 bn, according to Finance Minister Manuel Chang. At its peak in 1998, foreign debt was $ 6 bn. Mozambique benefited from debt cancellation under the HIPC and Multilateral Debt Relief Initiative programmes: the World Bank cancelled $ 1.3 bn, AfDB $ 500 m and the IMF $ 154 m, Chang said. Chang also pointed to the rapid increase in the government's domestic debt, which more than doubled between 2005 and 2008.

Mozambique failed to meet its target under the Ottawa treaty to demine the country by the end of 2008. *Mines* were planted during three different wars, and the national demining institute estimates that it will take six more years to clear them. However, there were only three land mine accidents, with seven victims, compared to 11 accidents and 24 victims the year before.

Mozambique in 2009

Frelimo's landslide victory in national elections confirmed its position as the predominant political party. Traditional opposition party Renamo continued its collapse, but a new third party made a strong showing. Donors withheld aid because of electoral misconduct and manipulation. Mozambique was not seriously affected by the global economic crisis. Economic growth continued, but poverty was not decreasing.

Domestic Politics

President Armando Guebuza was re-elected and the ruling Frelimo party won a landslide victory in the 28 October *elections*. However, the elections were controversial and tainted. EU observers concluded that "Frelimo's overwhelming victory suggests that the results reflect the choice of a vast majority of Mozambican voters." But the EU went on to say, "The broader electoral process was weakened by the insufficient measures of transparency shown by the country's electoral authorities, by an unlevel playing field during the electoral campaign and by limitations with regard to voter choice at local level." The lack of a level playing field and the growing role of Frelimo as the dominant party led the group of 19 budget support donors to withhold some aid late in the year in an attempt to force changes in Mozambican law.

There were three elections the same day, for president, national parliament and new provincial parliaments. Guebuza was re-elected, having received 75% of the vote; Renamo president Afonso Dhlakama, standing for the fourth time, gained 16%; Daviz Simango for the Mozambique Democratic Movement (MDM)

 | DOI 10.1163/9789004301122_007

had 9%. For the national parliament (Assembly of the Republic [AR]), Frelimo won 191 seats (more than a two-thirds majority), Renamo 51, and the MDM eight. Frelimo won majorities in all ten of the new provincial assemblies, gaining 703 of 812 seats; Renamo won 83, the MDM 24, and the 'Partido para a Paz, Democracia e Desenvolvimento' (PDD) two. Turnout was 45% of registered voters, similar to 2004 and much below the high levels of 1994 and 1999; 9.9 m, people registered to vote – over 90% of voting age adults. The MDM was a new party, formed in 2009. Simango had been the successful Renamo mayor of Beira, but was not chosen by Renamo to stand again; he had stood as an independent in the 2008 local elections and was overwhelmingly re-elected, but was then expelled from Renamo. Still tightly controlled by Dhlakama, who seemed to be losing interest and failed to organise effective election campaigns, Renamo seemed in terminal decline. Simango created the new party, the MDM, which largely attracted the more dynamic people from Renamo, plus some younger urban voters (it took one parliamentary seat for Maputo city from Frelimo). It was widely considered that with less than a year to organise, the MDM did well to gain 9% of the vote and eight AR seats, and could represent a much bigger challenge to Frelimo in the 2013 and 2014 elections.

Mozambique had been tinkering since 1994 with its *elections laws*, which were now confused and contradictory. A further law passed on 8 April clarified some problems, but also created new contradictions, particularly in the electoral calendar, and unexpectedly increased to six the number of documents that candidates for parliament had to present. Mozambique's election laws have always given the National Elections Commission (CNE) total freedom to act in secret, and even to change the results without explanation. This had been repeatedly criticised by domestic and international observers, but was never changed. The election procedure was an odd mixture of transparent and secret. Each polling station had a single register of up to 1,000 voters, the count was carried out in the polling station in the presence of observers and press as soon as polls closed, and the results were posted on the polling station door. This allowed parallel counts, and three were carried out – an accurate sample survey by a local NGO, the Electoral Observatory; a reasonably close tally taken by Radio Mozambique simply by reading out results all day during the day after polling; and a parallel count by election officials themselves. These parallel counts prevented the CNE from tampering too much with the results in secret, but other actions caused growing discontent. For example, full lists of candidates and of polling stations were never published.

Observers estimated that polling station staff were guilty of misconduct or *fraud* in at least 6% of polling stations. Ballot box stuffing in favour of Frelimo and Guebuza occurred in Tete, Niassa and Gaza provinces – in many cases polling stations claimed a 100% turnout with nearly everyone voting for Frelimo. The CNE (in secret and without comment) excluded 104,000 votes – 16% of the votes in Tete and 9% of the votes in Niassa – apparently because of impossibly high turnouts. The other widespread fraud took the form of polling station staff adding an extra ink mark or fingerprint to ballot papers for the opposition, making is seem as if the voter selected two candidates, thus invalidating the vote. The second ink mark was often in different coloured ink and the difference was obvious to journalists and observers when invalid votes were being reconsidered by the CNE. At a few polling stations, more than 30% of the votes cast were invalid, compared with a national average of 4%. Although ballot box stuffing and nullifying ballot papers is a crime, no action was taken against polling station staff and the evidence was destroyed by the CNE.

Although Frelimo's overwhelming victory was unquestioned, there were growing complaints by observers, diplomats and the local independent press of the lack of a *'level playing field'*. The CNE was seen as being biased toward Frelimo, and it excluded MDM parliamentary candidates lists for seven out of 11 provinces on the grounds that the MDM had not completed the new, more stringent conditions for its candidates in those provinces. Again, detailed reasons were kept secret. The issue went to the Constitutional Council, which ruled in favour of the CNE on the basis of secret CNE documents not disclosed to the MDM – but which were later shown to contain errors. During the campaign, there were widespread media reports and complaints about Frelimo using state cars in the campaign, and of teachers, health workers and other civil servants being put under heavy pressure to campaign for Frelimo. This followed a period when civil servants complained about growing pressure to join the party, and administrators were being pushed to favour Frelimo members for jobs, grants, licences and other forms of preferential treatment. Mozambique's First Lady, Maria da Luz Guebuza, was given increasing prominence, playing a part in her husband's election campaign, speaking at various international meetings, and being given prizes by obscure international organisations.

Mozambique's Central Office for the Fight against *Corruption* (GCCC) and the 11 provincial attorney's offices investigated 534 allegations of corruption and theft of state funds and property, according to GCCC director Ana Maria Gemo. Of these, 27 came to trial, 40 were shelved, and charges were laid in 155 cases; 111 people were arrested. The figures show a significant rise since the shake-up in mid-2007, when Augusto Paulino was named attorney general and named Gemo to head the GCCC. The trial of former transport minister Antonio Munguambe and Diodino Cambaza, former chair of the Mozambique Airports Company, began in November. They were accused of stealing $ 3 m. Former interior minister Almerino Manhenje remained in detention awaiting trial on corruption charges. A range of other corruption cases also became public. In Cabo Delgado province, $ 3.5 m were stolen from the government in at least seven different cases. Former provincial director of planning and finance Paulo Risco and four other finance officials were arrested. Tete provincial Director of Planning and Finances Jose Joao, and three senior officials, were arrested in August for stealing $ 5.4 m. Five staff members from the Manica planning and finance directorate were arrested and several provincial directors were dismissed; two civil servants in the education department were dismissed for stealing $ 38,000. Jose Carlos Amade, who had been administrator of Angoche, and before that of Muecate district, was expelled from the civil service; he had been publicly criticised in both districts for giving contracts to businesses owned by his family. The former permanent secretary of the ministry of health, Filomena Zimba, was arrested for corruption. In Matola, four officials were suspended for stealing $ 58,000 – 17% of the municipality's entire revenue for the year.

Mozambique still ranked 130th out of 180 countries in TI's Corruption Perception Index. A British construction firm, Mabey and Johnson (M&J) pleaded guilty in a London court to systematically bribing officials around the world to win lucrative contracts. One official of M&J said it had bribed Carlos Fragoso, who at the time was national director of roads and bridges in the ministry of public works. M&J said it paid £ 287,000 into his Swiss bank account between 14 October 1997 and 10 April 2000. Fragoso denied he had taken bribes and there has been no follow-up in Mozambique, where it is widely believed the money went to the Frelimo party rather than to Fragoso personally. The dropping of charges in May meant that no one was tried over the ruinous management of Banco Austral in 1998–2000 by people with important links in Frelimo, nor was anyone charged with the 11 August 2001 assassination of Antonio Siba-Siba Macuacua, the Bank of Mozambique head of banking supervision, who tried to clean up Banco Austral. However, Anibalzinho, the convicted killer of investigative journalist Carlos Cardoso, who was allowed to escape (for the third time) from a high security jail on 7 December 2008, was recaptured in South Africa in August.

In order to reduce conflicts of interest within the AR, it passed regulations requiring MPs to declare any personal or family interests they had in matters under debate, including cases where an MP or a close relative of an MP was involved in any business that would be affected by a law or resolution passed by the AR. However, MPs were still permitted to vote on matters in which they had an interest, and the AR did not establish a register of members' interests.

At the swearing-in ceremony for his second term, Guebuza said he was "launching a centralised mechanism to drive a successful *decentralisation* for local government, where the district serves as our development pole". In December, the government had already announced a series of changes to speed decentralisation. The Local Initiative Investment Budget (OIIL) had, since 2006, given each of the 128 districts at least $ 300,000 per year for locally decided projects to improve food security, create jobs and generate local income. This was money that was meant to be repaid, but the repayment rate had been low, both because of recipients' difficulties in making payments, and also because district administrations had no means to administer such funds. Formal District Development Funds had therefore been established to replace the OIIL. These were to be rotating loan funds, using both the $ 300,000 annual grant and repayments of previous loans. Funds were managed by the provincial governments, but the District Consultative Councils continued to play a key role in decision making. As further support, the existing Economic Rehabilitation Support Fund was redirected to work with micro-credit and banking institutions to expand financial services in the countryside. In July, as part of its programme to raise the quality of local administration, the government began raising by 25%–45% the salaries of state employees with high or mid-level education who were not working in the cities.

A new 2.4 km bridge over the Zambezi River linking Sofala and Zambezia provinces was opened in July. The $ 113 m bridge replaced an erratic ferry service. The bridge finally made it possible to drive from the north to the south of the country. As well as the psychological importance of physically linking the north and south, it was likely to increase internal trade.

Social *violence* continued in the poorest areas, reflecting a distrust of the better off and outsiders. Lynching of suspected criminals continued in urban neighbourhoods. Mobs attacked police stations near Maputo and Beira to try to take out and lynch an alleged murderer and a kidnapper. In Nicoadala district of Zambezia, local people accused the government of locking up the rain and giving it only to better off people; in February, 25 houses were burned down, three people were killed and six injured, accused of diverting the rain. Cholera is endemic, but in the poorest areas local people blamed the government and the better-off for spreading cholera to kill the poor, particularly through the use of a white powder. In northern Cabo Delgado province, mobs attacked cholera treatment tents, health workers and community leaders in January and November; on 11 November, police shot and killed four people in a crowd attacking a treatment centre in the village of Muadja, in Ancuabe district. In Quinga, Mogincual district, Nampula, a very poor area with high levels of malnutrition, a Red Cross volunteer was beaten to death in March. Three days later, health workers were attacked and, when the police defended them, the mob attacked the police with knives and spears, disembowelling and killing a police sergeant and seriously injuring two other policemen. A Red Cross activist was assaulted, buried up to her neck, and nearly murdered, when a mob demanded that she hand over "the cholera" she was allegedly keeping in her house. She was rescued by the police, who were attacked by the mob. Frightened police arrested 29 people and packed them into a tiny police cell in Mogincual, where 12 suffocated to death in the early morning of 17 March. Two police officers were each sentenced to one year in jail for actions leading to the deaths.

Foreign Affairs

Mozambique is one of the most *aid*-dependent countries in the world, so foreign relations are dominated by aid. OECD DAC figures for 2008, released during the year, showed that Mozambique received $ 1,994 m in aid (19% of GDP). The largest donors and lenders were the World Bank ($ 280 m), the United States ($ 227 m), the United Kingdom ($ 198 m), the EU ($ 161 m), Sweden ($ 120 m), the Netherlands ($ 106 m), Norway ($ 97 m), Denmark ($ 87 m), Canada ($ 77 m), Spain ($ 78 m), Germany ($ 75 m), and Ireland ($ 74 m).

Mozambique has been in the forefront of the donor shift to *budget support,* in which money is given directly to the government budget in exchange for detailed donor involvement in policy making and the writing of the budget. A quarter of aid is budget support ($ 465 m in 2008, which was 29% of government current expenditure). The group of 19 budget support donors, known as the G19 or Programme Aid Partners, had become the major interlocutor with the government on policy issues – to the annoyance of the United States and Japan, who are not members. A new agreement between the G19 and the government was signed on 29 April, but there were signs of tension. The government failed to keep its promises on justice and governance issues, and the G19 chair and Irish Ambassador Frank Sheridan warned that the conduct of upcoming elections would be an important test. On 28 May, the G19 pledged $ 472 m in budget support for 2010. The World Bank and Canada promised significant increases, but Sweden, which had supported Frelimo since before independence, made a token 3% cut in budget support as a protest at what it saw as the government's unwillingness to combat corruption. At the announcement press conference, G19 chair Sheridan said that several more of the donors had decided not to increase their budget support because of poor performance by the Mozambican government on governance issues. Donor tolerance on this had been partly due to Mozambique's rapid economic growth and claimed substantial reductions in poverty. On 15 September, the G19 issued an unusually strong statement criticising the exclusion of the MDM from standing in many provinces in the October elections, and then demanded and held angry meetings with CNE President Joao Leopoldo da Costa and Guebuza. Finally, in mid-December, the G19 stopped dispersing budget support (although continuing to disperse other aid). The *aid moratorium* was not solid – two large budget support donors, the World Bank and the EU, had released their money earlier, while three southern European countries who only made token budget support contributions (Portugal, Spain and Italy) did not adhere to the withholding of funds, which had the full backing of other influential donors, including the Nordics, Britain, Ireland, Switzerland and the Netherlands. The G19 demanded government commitments to rapid electoral law reform, tighter conflict of interest legislation, improved governance, and a reduction of the party's role in the state, particularly a ban on party cells in ministries. The government responded by taking a hard line, and the stand-off continued.

Mozambique was elected chair of the *SADC* Troika for Politics, Defence and Security in September, and was involved in unsuccessful negotiations in Maputo to try to resolve internal conflicts over disputed elections and governments in Lesotho, Zimbabwe and Madagascar. Former Mozambican transport minister Tomas Salomão was elected on 9 September for a second term as executive secretary of SADC.

Links with Brazil, Portugal and China all increased during the year, although China remained a relatively small player. Agreement was reached with *Brazil* on a number of projects, including the $ 100 m conversion of the former military air base at Nacala into a commercial airport. In September, Portugal signed agreements to the value of $ 1 bn with Mozambique, half for the creation of an investment bank. Guebuza visited Brazil in July.

Mozambique controversially signed an *interim EPA* with the EU on 16 June. The signing split SADC, as only Botswana, Lesotho and Swaziland signed, while others continued to negotiate. EPAs have been criticised because, although they allow duty-free and quota-free access to the European market, signatories must grant the EU access to their markets.

Socioeconomic Developments

Economic growth remained high, but fell to 6.1% compared with 6.7% in 2008 and an average of 7.8% in the five years up to 2007. Growth was significantly above earlier IMF projections of 4.5%, suggesting Mozambique had not been badly hit by the global economic crisis. Tax collection was $ 1.7 bn, which was 17.8% of GDP, up from 12.4% in 2004, reported Finance Minister Manuel Chang. The inflation rate in 2009 was 4.2%, the lowest recorded in the past ten years, according to the Bank of Mozambique. This compared with an inflation rate of 6.2% in 2008. The money supply grew by 34.3% over the year, partly because of increased credit to the private sector, and partly because of state financial operations. In December, net international reserves stood at $ 1.8 bn. Over the year the metical depreciated by 9.6% against the dollar. The IMF approved a credit for MZN 114 m Special Drawing Rights (SDRs) under the Fund's Exogenous Shocks Facility, and MZN 100 m in SDRs were disbursed. Subsidies kept fuel prices pegged at March levels despite large rises in oil prices, and cost $ 34 m. The G19 publicly criticised the subsidy in September, claiming it largely benefitted the better-off, who had big cars, and the subsidy was to be ended in early 2010.

Energy and mining played a central role in the economy. Exports for 2008, announced on 2 April, totalled $ 2,650 m. $ 1,450 m were from the Mozal aluminium smelter, which used Mozambican electricity but contributed little to the economy or tax base. Statistics were unclear, but 'other', most of which was titanium, came next at $ 442 m. Next was Cahora Bassa dam electricity, at $ 221 m, followed by gas at $ 152 m, both exported to South Africa. So the mineral-energy sector accounted for 85% of Mozambican exports. Agriculture and fishing exports included tobacco ($ 132 m), sugar ($ 71 m), cotton ($ 48 m), prawns ($ 45 m), and cashews ($ 23 m). Titanium mining in the north was highly successful, but BHP Billeton cancelled a proposed titanium heavy sands mine in Chibuto, Gaza.

New developments also took place in energy-linked sectors, notably *tree planting and biofuels*. Potential investments of $ 6 bn were approved, but Mozambique did not publish lists of how many were actually carried out. More than half were for three huge forestry projects in the north. Norwegian-owned Lurio Green Resources said it would invest $ 2.2 bn in 126,000 hectares of eucalyptus trees in Nampula province. The Portuguese-owned Portucel planned a 173,000 hectares eucalyptus plantation in Zambezia province. Both planned to set up paper mills. At least 14 biofuel projects were approved. In August, Enerterra, a Portuguese company, was granted 18,920 hectares in Cheringoma, Sofala, for the production of jatropha. Zambezi Grown Energy, with Mozambican, Asian and South African interests, was granted 15,000 hectares in Chemba district, Sofala, for sugar cane for energy. Both planned to export 90%, particularly to Europe, and sell 10% locally. Principle Energy was given 18,000 hectares in Manica province for sugar cane for ethanol. The Portuguese Galpenergia was developing sunflower and jatropha production in Sofala. British-owned Sun biofuels had 5,000 hectares in Manica province on which it was growing jatropha, and profitability was dependent on carbon credits. Meanwhile, a project for a 30,000-hectares sugar plantation for ethanol in Gaza province was cancelled; despite approval in 2007, work had not started, probably because lower oil prices made biofuels less attractive. The project was controversial because it diverted water from potential rice production.

Large natural gas reserves were found off the coast of northern Mozambique in the Rovuma basin, increasing the expectations that *oil* would be found there. Ten multinational oil companies carrying out oil exploration had spent $ 330 m since 2006. Development of huge *coal* mines in Tete moved forward. The Australian Riversdale Mining planned to start mining and processing coal in 2011. Its Benga mine would initially produce 5.3 m tonnes of raw coal a year, to be processed into about 1.7 m tonnes of top quality hard coking coal, plus 0.3 m tonnes of thermal coal per year for export. Coal that could not be exported would be burned in a 2,000 MW power station to be built next to the mine. The Brazilian mining giant Vale hoped to produce 8.5 m tonnes of coking coal and 2.5 m tonnes of thermal coal a year; low quality coal would be burned in a 600 MW power station. The rehabilitated Sena railway line from Tete to Beira port did not have the capacity to move all the coal that would be mined so, in October, Vale signed an agreement for a new railway line to Nacala port; 100 km of this line would run though Malawi. Meanwhile, the Sena railway itself, after four years of rehabilitation, was opened as far as the sugar mill at Marromeu, and Mutarara on the north bank of the Zambezi, and should reopen to serve the coal mines in 2010. The Sena line was destroyed in the war in the 1980s; in some areas Renamo rebels forced local people to pull up many kilometres of track by hand.

In May, Mozambique was accepted as candidate country for the Extractive Industries Transparency Initiative (EITI), and a coordinating committee was set up, consisting of four representatives of the government, four from civil society, and four from mining and oil companies. Under the EITI, all revenue received by governments, and all payments made by companies resulting from mining and hydrocarbon exploitation, are made public.

Huge investments in the minerals-energy sector and substantial GDP growth did not reduce *poverty*. The self-evaluation report of the National Forum for the APRM, published in March, asserted that the principle beneficiaries of growth were a tiny group and "the most credible indicators show an increase in absolute terms in the number of people below the minimum subsistence line". The National Forum is an establishment body of 58 people, including three provincial governors, the governor of the Bank of Mozambique, university rectors and representatives of eight parliamentary commissions, civil society and the private sector, and it explicitly rejected government and donor claims of dramatic reductions in poverty. "Mozambique's present development model, based on free individual initiative and the principles of a economic liberalism", was seen as creating unemployment and leaving many families without even enough to survive, especially in urban areas. This was polarising society, and created "serious risks" of conflict. In a survey, half of the respondents saw unemployment as the most serious threat to peace, stability and security, the peer review domestic forum noted. Towards the end of the year, internal government evaluations of the poverty reduction strategy programme 2006–2009 (PARPA II) showed that median incomes were falling and poverty was actually increasing. In particular, the goal of increasing rural incomes by improving agricultural technology had been a complete failure; over 90% of Mozambican farmers are peasants using only a hoe and no fertiliser or improved seeds. Most did not grow enough to feed themselves adequately for the entire year. A measure of this was that the number of children with chronic malnutrition (stunting, measured as height for age) only fell from 48% in 2003 to 44% in 2008, still "very high" by WHO standards, according to the 2008 Multi-Indicator Cluster Survey, published in 2009. Meanwhile, the under-five mortality rate was falling slowly, from 201 per 1,000 live births in 1997, to 153 in 2003, and to 138 in 2008, as announced in October. Zambezia province had the highest under-five mortality rate with 205 deaths per 1,000 live births, while the rate in the capital, Maputo city, with the best health services in the country, was 103.

Health Minister Ivo Garrido reported that, at 4,000 deaths, *malaria* death rates were 25% lower than in 2008, but with 4 m cases per year, malaria remained the main public health problem, more serious than HIV/AIDS. Malaria was responsible for 40% of out-patient consultations and 60% of paediatric hospital admissions. The malaria death rate was falling as a result of household spraying, better testing available at the local level, and the use of insecticide-treated bed nets; 2 m insecticide-treated bed nets had been distributed, and over the coming three years 6 m more would be made available – still not enough for the entire population. The *HIV* prevalence rate in Mozambique was 15% for people aged between 15 and 49, down from 16% in 2007, meaning that "the stabilization plateau has been reached," said Garrido. These figures indicated that about 1.6 m Mozambicans were infected with HIV, and that over 120,000 new infections occurred annually. Antiretroviral drugs were available in every district in the country, and about 160,000 Mozambicans were taking such drugs. The HIV prevalence rate was highest in the south, at 21%, followed by 18% in the centre. In the three northern provinces (Nampula, Niassa and Cabo Delgado) it was 9%; rates were lower than in neighbouring countries. The method used to estimate the prevalence rate was testing the blood of pregnant women for HIV antibodies at 36 sentinel sites located in all 11 provinces. Cholera continued to be endemic, with 20,000 cases and 155 deaths during the year. At least 103 people died of hunger in the year ending 31 March, according to Deputy National Director of Agricultural Services Marcelo Chaquisse.

Poor rainfall in the south and centre of the country in the first half of the rainy season (October to December) caused widespread crop failure; the south is already traditionally dryer and was predicted to be more affected by climate change. The more productive northern provinces had a normal rainfall. Tobacco became Mozambique's biggest *agricultural export*, rising to 43,000 tonnes, compared with 39,000 tonnes in 2008. Mozambique Leaf Tobacco employed 4,000 workers in their processing factory in Tete, and had 120,000 contract farmers in Tete, Zambezia and Niassa provinces.

The electricity grid reached 94 of the 128 districts; 42 districts had been linked to the grid since 2003. Minimum wages were agreed on 28 April, ranging from $ 55 per month for agricultural workers to $ 114 per month in the financial sector. The banking network was slowly expanding. There were 352 bank branches, but 56% were in the three largest cities – Maputo, Beira and Nampula. Half of all Automatic Teller Machines (ATMs) were in Maputo, and 71% of establishments that accepted payment by bank debit or credit card were in Maputo.

In a bid to encourage tourism and raise taxes, parliament approved a law relaxing restrictions on gambling and allowing *casinos* throughout the country, with the proviso that they be linked to hotels rated at least four-star. The law also legalised on-line gambling and slot machines in places that were not part of the casinos.

Education expansion continued, with 1,200 new classrooms built in 2009, of which 1,137 were for first level primary schools. This was below the target of 1,400 classrooms per year; and an early target of 6,000 per year had already been abandoned because of shortages of building materials and skilled labour. The teacher-pupil ratio was 1:65. Managing director of Mozambique's National Prison System, Joao Zandamela, said in August that most of the 119 jails in the country were overcrowded. There were 13,453 detainees at that time, 4,704 of whom were awaiting trial.

Results were announced for the August 2007 national *census*. The resident population then was 20,226,296, up from 16.1 m in the 1997 census – an increase of 28%. Mozambicans did not seem to be moving to cities – the urban population was 29.8% of the total, almost identical to the 28.6% in 1997. Nampula remained the largest province, with 4 m people, followed by Zambezia with 3.8 m, and Tete with 1.8 m. The census found that 46.9% of the population were under 15 years old, 50.1% were between 15 and

64, and only 3.1% were 65 or older. The fertility rate remained unchanged at an average of 5.8 children per woman. Illiteracy fell from 60.5% of the population aged 15 and above in 1997, to 50.4% in 2007; 34.6% of men were illiterate compared with 64.2% of women.

Climate had been changing for the past 45 years, according to a detailed study by the National Disasters Management Institute. Between 1960 and 2005, temperatures rose by an average of between 1.1 and 1.6 degrees (centigrade). The rainy season was starting later than it used to. In some parts of northern Mozambique the rains began 45 days later than was the case half a century ago. Cyclones were becoming more frequent and more intense. Between 1980 and 1993, Mozambique was hit by four cyclones, one of which had wind speeds in excess of 100 km an hour, while between 1994 and 2007, there were 11 cyclones, six of which were more devastating than any in the preceding period.

Mozambique in 2010

Riots over the rising cost of living came days before a national survey showed that poverty levels had not fallen for six years – the first term of President Armando Guebuza. No one questioned his overwhelming victory for a second and final term in late 2009, but early 2010 brought a flurry of criticism from observers and donors over the conduct of the election, leading to a brief donor strike. Drug smuggling and its links to the ruling party also became an issue.

Domestic Politics

Growing poverty dominated domestic politics in the second half of the year. On 1–3 September, *demonstrations* against the high cost of living in the capital Maputo closed the city and left 13 dead and 300 injured. Government responded by reversing some price rises and subsidising the price of bread. In Maputo and neighbouring Matola, young people, coordinated by mobile telephone text message (SMS), blocked all main roads with burning tyres and other barriers on 1 September. There was some looting of shops and market stalls, and cars and buses were attacked. There were also disturbances in the Beira corridor (Beira, Chimoio, Gondola and Vila Manica). Police spokesman Pedro Cossa said repeatedly that the police were only using rubber bullets and not live ammunition, but in another example of Mozambique's press freedom, the government newspaper 'Noticias' quoted Natércia Duarte, clinical director of Hospital Geral José Macamo in Maputo, saying that 43 of those admitted had been shot by firearms. The Electoral Observatory, a coalition of civil society groups including the main

 | DOI 10.1163/9789004301122_008

religious denominations, called the demonstrations "a popular revolt against the established order" and said they were caused by poverty and hunger. There were also complaints by demonstrators about the growing ostentation of the better off, with ever-bigger houses and cars. In September, the government released the third national family expenditure survey ('Inquérito aos Orçamentos Familiares'; IOF), which showed that the percentage of the population living below the poverty line had not changed in six years – it was 54% in the 2002–3 survey and 55% in the 2008–9 survey.

Annual *inflation* at the time of the riots was 17%, but the Bank of Mozambique reported that the prices of fruit and vegetables had risen by 34% in the first half of 2010 – in part because a substantial amount of food is imported from South Africa and the Mozambican Metical depreciated significantly against the South African Rand – from 3.7 Mt to the Rand at the start of the year to 5 Mt to the Rand at the time of the riot. This highlighted the fact that Maputo food was being imported from South Africa instead of being produced domestically, which raised fundamental questions about development policy.

Frelimo and President Armando Guebuza had won an overwhelming victory in the 28 October 2009 elections, and when he resumed office in January, Guebuza made few *changes in the government*. Education Minister Aires Aly became prime minister, replacing Luisa Diogo, while Zeferino Martins became education minister. Iolanda Cintura became minister of women's affairs and social welfare. Carmelite Namashalua was named minister of state administration. In October, following the riots, Guebuza sacked the ministers for agriculture, industry and health. Interior Minister and Frelimo Political Commission member Jose Pacheco was moved to agriculture; Armando Inronga was named trade and industry minister, Alberto Mondlane became interior minister, and Alexandre Manguele was named health minister. In parliament, Veronica Macamo was named speaker. Parliament also changed its rules to allow the third party in parliament, the 'Movimento Democrático de Moçambique' (MDM), to have a formal party bench, even though it had only eight seats. Renamo had 51 seats (its lowest total in four elections) and Frelimo 191.

Foreign Affairs

No one doubted the collapse of the opposition and overwhelming victory of Frelimo and President Armando Guebuza in the 28 October 2009 elections. But ballot box stuffing, deliberate invalidation of ballot papers, and incompetence and secrecy by the National Elections Commission ('Comissão Nacional de Eleições'; CNE) drew criticism from domestic observers and the Constitutional Council, which validated the election on 27 December 2009. The *international donor community* continued to pursue the issue in early 2010. The Commonwealth hit at the selection process of the CNE, which gave an impression of bias, and at the CNE's lack of transparency. In February, the EU observers issued their report and criticised the lack of transparency, the unlevel playing field, and legislation that made it practically impossible to make a complaint.

The Group of 19 (G19) *budget support donors* felt they had been snubbed by the CNE at a meeting during the elections and were angered by what they saw as the unfair exclusion of some MDM candidates. This compounded donor concerns about government unwillingness to act on justice, corruption and conflict of interest. In mid-December 2009, the G19 budget support donors suddenly launched a strike, refusing to release budget support funds until the government took action on these issues (although other aid was released on schedule). The decision was unexpected and the timing was odd, because it was between the election and the installation of the new government – perhaps as a way to remind the new government of donor power in Mozambique. Donor and lender money accounted for 44% of the 2010 budget, according to Planning and Development Minister Aíuba Cuereneia, so the donor strike mattered. But support was not total – the EU and the World Bank are both G19 members, but they released money early, before the strike formally started – so the strike only began to have an impact in March. The donors had not announced the strike, but the government did, on 6 March. By then donors were becoming worried; the financial year of one European donor ends in the first week of April, and they needed to disperse funds in March. The strike collapsed in mid-March; donors having accepted a letter from the government that said the government was already doing what the donors wanted.

Donors, observers and government all agreed that election laws needed to be reviewed. The government had been minded to accept a civil society proposal for quite broad consultation and the writing of a completely new electoral code in 2011. Surprisingly, donors were not enthusiastic, and one key donor official, who was leaving his post in August, wanted action before he left. So the major government concession to end the donor strike was to not carry out a broad consultation or write an entirely new code, as called for by civil society and electoral observers, but rather to simply revise the existing law with little public consultation, which was started in mid-year.

Government anger at the donor strike exploded in the 4 May government evaluation of donor performance, published as part of the annual budget support donor-government Aide-Mémoire. In an unprecedented *attack on the donors*, the government said discussions with donors "often degenerated into mutual accusations, suggesting that at some point the relationship between [the government and donors] ceased to be a partnership". The government continued: "The partners surprisingly tried to change the dynamic of 2010 commitments according to their perception of what happened in 2009 [and their view of] the need for the GoM to change the electoral law, improve transparency in economic governance, [and] accelerate the legal reform." This was in the name of political dialogue, but this dialogue currently appeared to be a cloak of confusion. The government asked: "at what levels can the 'political dialogue' be made, with whom, when and on what, and how to integrate it positively in the partnership's framework?"

The annual Aide-Mémoire also contained an independent evaluation of donor performance. In interviews for the evaluation, government was sharply critical of donors. One official was quoted as saying: "It seems that any technical staff on the side of the partners can make political dialogue at any time, which is not admissible. Technical staff may not engage in this kind of dialogue, much less try to give instructions to national directors and ministers." Another argued: "Partners continue to involve themselves in certain areas where they have no technical qualifications. Therefore, they want impossible things done in impossible times. Sometimes the dialogue is undermined by a lack of technical capacity to understand the questions. There is no coherence and unity among the donors on technical questions, with some saying one thing and others wanting something else."

A further issue was the very large number of *donor missions*. The G19 sent 167 missions in 2009, which took up huge amounts of government time. On the government side, the arrogance of donors had simply become too much. But donors, too, were angry. In their part of the joint Aide-Mémoire they said they "consider the performance on governance as unsatisfactory". Aid to Mozambique had been increasing, and it remained very high, but the increase stopped. Aid was not increased for 2010 and two donors cut their budget support, Switzerland by 40% and Sweden by a token 2%.

Aid to Mozambique remained the same in 2009 as in 2008, at exactly $ 2 bn, according to data released by OECD in early 2011. Donors and lenders of over $ 50 m were: USA ($ 256 m), World Bank ($ 213 m), EU ($ 205 m), IMF ($ 153 m), Germany ($ 114 m), Denmark ($105m), the Netherlands ($99m), Sweden ($99m), Norway ($80m), Canada ($ 75 m), AfDB ($ 75 m), Spain ($ 69 m), Portugal ($ 68 m), Ireland ($ 64 m), Japan ($ 61 m), UK ($ 55 m). Meanwhile, the *United States* directly intervened in Mozambican politics. On 1 June, President Barack Obama named as a "drug kingpin" Mohamed Bachir Suleman (MBS), one of Mozambique's most prominent and wealthy businessmen. The designation made it illegal for US citizens and businesses to conduct financial or commercial transactions with him or three of his businesses: Grupo MBS Limitada, Grupo MBS – Kayum Centre, and Maputo Shopping Centre. The US Department of the Treasury said that Mohamed Bachir Suleman was a large-scale narcotics trafficker, asserting that his network contributed to the growing trend of narcotics trafficking and related money laundering across southern Africa, and was centred on his family-owned business conglomerate Grupo MBS Limitada. MBS is close to Frelimo and the respected independent weekly 'Savana' reported that he had donated $ 1 m to the Frelimo electoral campaign in 2009. Government said little except to claim the US had not provided any evidence for its claim.

Mozambique has been an important *heroin transit* and warehousing centre for more than a decade. Heroin is shipped from Pakistan to northern Mozambique, brought ashore in small boats, then warehoused (particularly in Nacala) and, when orders are received, shipped out in containers from Mozambican and South African ports. This was first publicly reported a decade ago, but the international community decided not to make an issue of it. Since then, large buildings have been built in Maputo and Nampula by people who have no obvious legal source for such wealth. Over the past decade there have been no heroin seizures and no public battles between groups of drug traders, suggesting that the heroin trade was tightly regulated by senior people in the government, police and military. Four cables released by *Wikileaks* show that Todd Chapman, US Chargé d'Affaires (acting ambassador) in Maputo (until he was posted to Afghanistan in May), made a wide range of serious and often false accusations against prominent Mozambicans. The cables were sent by Chapman in July and November 2009 and January 2010. The jumble of accurate and false information is shown by the part of the cables dealing with drug trading. Chapman notes the "close relationship" between MBS and both Guebuza and former president Joaquim Chissano, which seems to be true. But Chapman went on to say that "the main drug organizations are rumored to support extremist Islamist elements in Mozambique", which seems totally false.

Hugely exaggerated claims were made about the Chinese, Indian and South African presence in Mozambique. Widespread publicity was given to totally spurious reports of hundreds of white South African farmers settling in Mozambique and of *China* investing billions of dollars and being given vast tracts of land. In fact, China had only a tiny presence. Mozambique's Investment Promotion Centre estimated Chinese business investment between 2000 and 2009 at $ 115 m, plus a number of construction projects including a new Maputo airport terminal and, in June, China promised further loans of $ 200 m, including a second phase of Maputo airport. In December, Tong Jian Investment Company of China signed a contract for a $ 200 m vehicle assembly plant and a $ 150 m hotel in Maputo. A proposal by Tong Jian for the development of the Katembe municipal district, on the opposite side of Maputo Bay from the centre of the city, was rejected because Tong Jian had wanted to build a complex for Chinese workers. Historically, Frelimo has never become dependent on one sponsor. During the liberation war, it won backing from both China and the Soviet Union. In recent years it joined both the British Commonwealth and the Portuguese equivalent, the 'Comunidade dos Países de Língua Portuguesa'. In dealing with foreign investors and partners, it is now following the same pattern, but its decisions are more commercial and less political. Former prime minister Luisa Diogo gave a talk on 24 November at the School of Oriental and African Studies, London, and said China had a "very specific manner" of cooperation, and thus was a "non-traditional partner". She said that traditional partners, such as Sweden and the UK, did programme and budget support and worked through NGOs. Japan was more project-oriented. The US did projects plus private sector programmes. China did not do budget support but did wider project support, such as building the new foreign ministry and high court. The US and Europe would not even look at such a project, but China would, she said. Similarly China supported infrastructure and was involved in dams, roads, airports, electricity and telecoms. But it was not all good, she continued. China wanted Mozambique to give some guarantees, such as natural resources, "which we cannot do under Mozambican law". Any use of natural resources – minerals, land, fish, timber – should be based on project proposals. She affirmed that, by law, Mozambique could not set aside resources for anyone, and Mozambique was very careful in following the laws.

The same issue caused a diplomatic incident with *India*, when Indian Coal Minister Sriprakash Jaiswal, who was accompanied by state-owned Coal India officials, at a meeting with Minister of Mineral Resources Esperanca Bias, made a request for a further five coal exploration licences in Tete. This was rejected on

10 January 2011 because Coal India already had two licences in Moatize, Tete, which it had not yet begun to exploit. There were also problems with India over the contract to upgrade the railway line from Beira port to the Tete coal mines, which should have been completed by September 2009, but had not been finished by the end of 2010, and there were major criticisms over the poor quality of the work. RICON, the company carrying out the upgrade, is a consortium of two Indian railway companies, Rites and Ircon. The chair of CFM, the Mozambican state railway and ports company, Rosario Mualeia, blamed the World Bank, saying the $ 104 m loan was conditional on the privatisation of the project but the state company CFM could have done a better job.

Socioeconomic Developments

The results of the 2008–9 IOF, which showed that the percentage of the population living below the *poverty* line had not changed in six years, and was 55% in the 2008–2009 survey, was not unexpected, following data from the 2008 rural income survey ('Trabalho de Inquérito Agricola') released earlier in the year. Officially, 70% of Mozambicans were classed as 'rural' and the 2008 survey showed that most rural Mozambicans were poorer in 2008 than they had been in 2002, and most rural Mozambicans had a cash income of less than $ 1 per week (most rural 'income' comes from the imputed value of self-produced food). Between 2002 and 2008, mean rural income rose while median rural income fell, which meant the better off were getting richer, but the poor majority were getting poorer. Also released during the year was a series of studies on the impact of the 2006–2009 Poverty Reduction Strategy, PARPA II ('Plano de Acção para a Redução da Pobreza Absoluta, 2006–2009'). They concluded that PARPA II had failed to enhance farmers' income and so poverty in rural Mozambique may have remained fairly constant. Neither had it increased agricultural production and productivity, and thus had not reduced poverty. Chronic malnutrition (low height for age) fell from 48% of children under five in 2003 to 44% in 2008, but remained 'very high' by WHO standards.

The failure to reduce poverty brought increasing criticism from economists of the government's development policy, which relies on foreign investment and the free market to end poverty. Eminent economists used speeches and newspaper articles during the year to call for more government support for economic sectors, particularly agriculture, but there was little response. In its 24 May "Letter of Intent" to the IMF, the government said it would concentrate on major projects and mining. Agriculture was mentioned only with respect to "social spending". Nothing was said about supporting Mozambican entrepreneurs. "The focus of the central government's investment strategy will be in transport and electricity infrastructure", the government told the IMF.

A damning study on the *agriculture* sector was completed in August by the ministry of finance inspectorate. It cited the Maputo Declaration of 2003, which said that 10% of government budgets should go to agriculture, and noted that in the 2009 budget, agriculture received only 3.3% of current expenses and 5.7% of investment. Information on the family sector was "non-existent" and there was no information on the impact of funds spent by the ministry. Extension services reached only 5% of farmers and reports exaggerated the impact of extension. Use of irrigation was very low, in part due to lack of training. "There do not exist packets of technologies locally appropriate and available." No *land concessions* of over 1,000 ha were approved in 2010, reversing a policy of large concessions for foreign investors wanting to plant biofuel crops and forests.

A key issue for the government was the *exchange rate*. From 2002 to 2008 the Metical was pegged at between 24 and 26 to the dollar, but from mid-2009 it began to be devalued, reaching 32 by April, then jumping to 37 Mt to the dollar by the time of riots in September, which were caused in part by the high cost of imported food. Faced with the riots, the Bank of Mozambique pulled the exchange rate back to 32 by the end of the year.

Mozambique has 11 different minimum wages, set in April each year. Those set in 2010 ranged from $ 49 per month for sugar workers to $ 82 for electricity and gas workers, and then a separate and much higher $ 108 for the finance sector (all at 32 Mt = $1).

Meanwhile, Mozambique was becoming a major *mineral-energy* exporter. It already exported gas and electricity to South Africa and significant amounts of titanium, but Tete province in west-central Mozambique had the world's largest untapped reserve of high quality coking coal. Both Vale of Brazil and Riversdale of Australia were developing mines and expected to begin exporting in 2011. In late 2010, Rio Tinto made an offer for Riversdale, which effectively valued its Tete reserves at $ 3 bn. India and China were both interested; Tata had a shareholding in Riversdale and India was undertaking coal exploration, but Mozambique was explicitly refusing to do political deals with India and China for exploration rights, saying that it was only interested in companies that were prepared to move forward to exploit the reserves. Extensive exploration for gas and oil had been going on for several years along the north coast near the border with Tanzania. Significant marketable quantities of gas had been found, but the oil was probably not exploitable.

The government confirmed its commitment to the Extractive Industries Transparency Initiative (EITI). A coordinating committee was set up, consisting of four representatives of the government, four from civil society, and four from mining and oil companies. Under the EITI, all revenue received by governments, and all payments made by companies, resulting from mining and hydrocarbon exploitation, are made public. The Frelimo party company SPI won the third *mobile telephone licence* in a consortium with a Vietnamese firm Vietel.

Mozambican *banks* made a 2009 profit of $ 143 m, according to the KPMG annual survey of the Mozambican banking sector, published on 23 February 2011. By far the largest and most profitable bank was Millennium BIM, earning half the sector's profits and having 37% of all national banking assets. BIM is 67% owned by BCP (Banco Comercial Português) Internacional and 26% by the Mozambican state and state-linked institutions. The second largest bank is BCI, which is 51% owned by the Portuguese state-owned Caixa Geral de Depósitos, 30% by Banco Português de Investimento, and 18% by the Mozambican group Insitec. The third largest bank is Standard Bank.

Corruption became a higher profile issue in Mozambique, with somewhat mixed consequences. Five people were convicted on 27 February of stealing 91 m Mt ($ 3 m) from the Mozambique Airports Company ('Aeroportos de Moçambique': ADM). Former transport minister Antonio Munguambe was sentenced to 20 years in jail, former ADM chair Diodino Cambaza was sentenced to 22 years, and former ADM financial director Antenor Pereira received 20 years. Maputo City Court Judge Dimas Marroa made clear that he was handing down exemplary sentences. "A large part of the state budget comes from donors, and we cannot allow this money to be stolen. We can't continue like this." He added: "I call on all those who manage the public sector to keep their hands off state money."

The man indirectly responsible for Joaquim Chissano's election victory in 1999 was jailed for 12 years on 7 December for stealing 3.6 m Mt ($ 100,000). Orlando Comé had been head of the government Data Processing Centre ('Centro do Processamento de Dados'; CPD). He was convicted of putting CPD money into his own bank account, and using CPD funds and credit cards for personal travel, school fees, dinners, house rent, and even casino spending. But Comé was better known as having been computer director for STAE, the technical secretariat of electoral administration in the CNE, for the 1994, 1999 and 2004 elections. Comé had remained as head despite complaints after every election of poorly written, untested and insecure computer programmes. It is believed that lack of computer security allowed results to be changed in 1999, ensuring the election of Joaquim Chissano as president. The 1999 election was very close, and at the 2004 elections when he was heading an observation mission, former US President Jimmy Carter publicly questioned the 1999 outcome. Comé was believed to have protection at the highest levels of the Chissano circle, and the director of STAE and president of the CNE had no control over him, and thus were unable to demand better computer systems. After Armando Guebuza took office as president in 2005, protection melted away. Comé was quickly dropped as computer director of STAE. Workers at the CPD began to publicly protest about Comé's mismanagement and corruption. In 2008, he was dismissed as head of CPD and in 2009 charged with corruption.

The largest tobacco buyer in Mozambique (and the world), Universal corporation (trading as Mozambique Leaf Tobacco, MLT), admitted paying bribes totalling $ 165,000 to "a governor in Mozambique" and to officials (and a brother and a wife of officials) in the ministry of agriculture between 2004 and 2007. On 6 August the company pleaded guilty to charges brought by the US Securities and Exchange Commission (SEC), and paid fines and penalties of $ 9 m. Between October 2005 and July 2006 MLT had paid cash to "a governor" and given "gifts including supplies for a bathroom renovation, personal travel on a company jet, and cash payments to officials in Mozambique". These payments related to the grant of an exclusive license to buy tobacco in Chifunde district, Tete – one of the best districts for tobacco. The SEC said that $ 86,830 in bribes relating to Chifunde had brought MLT an extra $ 457,260 in profits in the first year alone. This was the second time a company had admitted bribing Mozambican officials. In September 2009, the British construction firm Mabey and Johnson (M&J) had pleaded guilty in a London court to giving Carlos Fragoso, then national director of roads and bridges in the Mozambican ministry of public works, $ 450,000 between 1997 and 2000. The money had been paid into a Swiss bank account. Other unnamed Mozambican roads officials had also been bribed, the company admitted. Despite companies admitting to bribing senior Mozambican officials, the Mozambican government made no comment, and took no action against those said to have received the bribes.

Orlando Jose, director of investigations, audit and intelligence of the Customs Service was gunned down outside his house on 26 April. He had been responsible for several very high profile customs raids in the previous weeks. On 21 April, a car was stopped heading for Zimbabwe with $ 400,000 in cash hidden in the door panel, apparently intended for the purchase of diamonds from Zimbabwe. On 26 April, just three hours before he was assassinated, Jose held a press conference promising a crackdown on smuggling, and he displayed three luxury cars that had been apprehended, one of which belonged to a powerful Nampula economic group. Jose had only been in the job for a year, and was challenging corrupt networks inside the customs service.

Cholera riots continued, with poor people, particularly in northern coastal areas, convinced that health workers and better off people were trying to poison them by putting cholera in the water, when in fact they were putting chlorine in the water to prevent cholera. In Gurue district, Zambezia province, where 19 people had died and 670 cases of cholera were registered, seven people were killed in disturbances.

Malaria remained the main cause of death, leading to 29% of all deaths, compared with 27% for HIV/AIDS, according to the National Survey on the Causes of Mortality in Mozambique published on 24 March by the National Statistics Institute. Perinatal illnesses accounted for 7% of deaths, diarrhoeal diseases 4%, pneumonia 4%, accidents and other "external causes" 4%, and tuberculosis (without HIV/AIDS as a contributing factor) 3%. The HIV prevalence rate was declining; it was 16% of people aged between 15 and 49 in 2004 and had fallen to 12% in 2010.

National Demining Institute director Julio Braga said that only 63 of the country's 128 districts could be declared free of mines. It was announced that *mine explosions* had killed 15 people and injured a further four in 2009. Under its project 'Transforming Guns into Hoes', the Christian Council of Mozambique had collected and destroyed 700,000 illegally held guns since 1995.

Somali pirates seized a Mozambican fishing boat in Mozambican waters on 27 December in their southernmost attack so far. The boat, Vega 5, was later turned into a mother ship to allow the pirates to work further afield. The crew consisted of 19 Mozambicans, three Indonesians and two Spaniards.

Mozambique in 2011

Little happened on the domestic political scene, apart from the notable performance of a new political party. Foreign policy played out mainly at the economic interface, with major foreign interests featuring prominently. Mozambique's leap to become a major mineral-energy exporter dominated its economic performance. By the end of the decade, the country is expected to be the largest exporter in Africa of natural gas, electricity and high quality metallurgical (coking) coal. But poverty was not reduced during the year and socio-economic disparities remained a major challenge.

Domestic Politics

Municipal by-elections served as an indicator of *shifting political trends*. The new opposition party, the Mozambique Democratic Movement (MDM), headed by Daviz Simango, mayor of Beira (not to be confused with David Simango, Frelimo mayor of Maputo), was taken seriously by the dominant party, Frelimo. Of the 43 elected mayors, 42 were Frelimo, which in July instructed five to resign. Two in the south where Frelimo was dominant refused. But those in Quelimane (Zambézia province), Pemba (Cabo Delgado) and Cuamba (Niassa) agreed, and by-elections were set for 7 December. It is probable that Frelimo thought that the three unpopular mayors would lose local elections in 2013, and decided to move before the MDM had time to build its organising capacity. Frelimo won two of the cities, but the MDM's Manuel de Araujo won 62% of the vote in Quelimane, making him an important political figure. Renamo did not stand in the municipal by-elections.

 | DOI 10.1163/9789004301122_009

Its president, Afonso Dhlakama, had moved to Nampula in the north, and little was heard of him – except for regular statements promising anti-government demonstrations that never took place. MDM head Daviz Simango had been expelled from Renamo by Dhlakama in 2008 and other key figures, including de Araujo, had left Renamo to join the MDM. Although Renamo was the second largest party in parliament, it was fading, and it was widely expected that the MDM would replace Renamo as the official opposition after the municipal elections in 2013 and national elections in 2014. Frelimo remained the dominant party, with good organisation and broad support. Nevertheless, patronage remained a key part of party and government, and there were complaints that Frelimo party membership was required for promotion in the civil service, loans from the district development fund, licences, etc. Businesses linked to President Armando Guebuza and Frelimo had an inside track on government contracts, and teachers in several places complained in the press about being forced to make contributions to Frelimo. MDM support initially came largely from disillusioned Renamo members. The test would be MDM's ability to gain support from an increasingly disaffected youth.

There is a two-term limit for the *state president* and Guebuza was half-way through his second term. In a manoeuvre that was never adequately explained, Frelimo had told parliament in 2010 that it wanted a special commission to make changes to the constitution, but refused to say what they were. There was widespread speculation that Guebuza and his allies were looking for a way to keep him in power, either by changing the two-term limit or by strengthening the post of prime minister for him, as had happened in Russia. But gossip from within the party said that the younger generation rejected any attempt to keep Guebuza in power, saying it was time for the post-liberation-war generation to take over. The 10th party congress was to be held in September 2012, and by year's end there was no clear favourite for the position of party president and national presidential candidate.

Frelimo is noted for its strong party unity; few people have ever been expelled from the party, and potential opposition figures have been co-opted, while splits and disagreements have generally not been allowed to spill over. However, there were many fault-lines with the party: between generations, with the young feeling marginalised; between regions and languages, with people from the centre and Nampula province feeling discriminated against by those from the south and the far north; between supporters of former president Chissano and Guebuza backers; and between those who saw the party as mainly for self-advancement and others who saw it as the best way to promote national development.

The *media* remained particularly free and often highly critical of government. Although the front page of the government owned daily 'Noticias' reflected a pro-Frelimo line, articles inside the newspaper, particularly reports from the districts, were frequently highly critical.

Parliament had decided that elections should always take place in the first two weeks of October, but there were sharp divisions between Frelimo and the opposition on a number of other *electoral issues*, including the size and composition of the National Electoral Commission and on means to reduce ballot box stuffing and other fraud within polling stations, which meant that parliament did not meet its September deadline for drafting a new electoral law. The total number of *districts* had been increased to 150 by splitting 13 large districts in half and by defining provincial capitals as districts.

Other domestic events included the publication of a revised highway code, which set a rural speed limit of 120 km/h and banned the use of hand-held mobile telephones while driving.

Over 800,000 guns and other items of military equipment had been collected since 1995 under the Mozambique Christian Council's "Transforming Guns into Hoes" programme. Mozambique's best know painter, Malangatana Valente Ngwenya, died on 3 January.

Foreign Affairs

The Mozambican leadership remained sympathetic to Robert Mugabe in Zimbabwe and Muammar Kadhafi in Libya, and former president Joaquim Chissano continued as the unsuccessful SADC negotiator in Madagascar. *SADC* elected Guebuza as its deputy president at its meeting in Luanda, Angola, on 18 August. The next annual summit would therefore be in Maputo, when Mozambique would take over the rotating presidency from Angola. But in practice, international issues were predominantly economic, often related to investment. Mozambique was late submitting its application for membership of the *Export Industries Transparency Initiative* and even then the application was incomplete and was rejected on 23 August.

Tensions continued with *Malawi* over transport. Malawi and coal mining company Rio Tinto wanted to use the Zambezi River for barges to carry cargo to the sea, but the government rejected these proposals on environmental grounds – the extensive dredging required would have too much impact on river flows, and there was a danger of pollution if a barge sank. Despite lack of agreement with Mozambique, Malawi completed the construction of an inland port at Nsanje on the Shire River, which it was not able to use.

The government continued to resist heavy pressure from the international community to renegotiate contracts for so-called *mega-projects*. The first three – the Mozal aluminium smelter, which uses Cahora Bassa electricity, the export of natural gas from

Inhambane to Sasol in South Africa, and the Kenmare titanium mine on the coast of Zambézia – benefitted from a wide range of tax and other incentives and contributed little to the Mozambican economy. Contracts agreed after 2007 had fewer incentives, but Mozambique did not gain much from the sharp rises in mineral and energy prices. An IMF staff report in May estimated that mega-projects and mining companies paid Mozambique only 5% of their profits, while they should have paid 30%. The IMF Executive Board, in a statement agreed on 24 May and published on 27 June, called on Mozambique to renegotiate mega-project contracts, and pointed out that other countries, including Peru and Tanzania, had renegotiated contracts. Economist Jeffrey Sachs, in a speech in Maputo on 13 January, also called for renegotiation of contracts. Mozambique Catholic bishops, in a pastoral letter on 20 June, said the mega-projects received "excessive" fiscal benefits and contracts should be renegotiated. But the government remained steadfastly opposed. The sale of the final 15% of Hydroelectrica de Cahora Bassa held by the Portuguese state was still delayed by disagreements over the price.

A *World Bank*-imposed privatisation of the central railways to an Indian company proved disastrous and was finally cancelled. Ricon was a consortium of two Indian companies, Rites and Ircon, and the World Bank gave a $ 104 m loan to upgrade the railway on condition that the Mozambican railways administration be kept at arms length. The project was essential to move coal from Tete to Beira port and should have been completed in 2009; the contact on the incomplete upgrading was finally cancelled.

The issue of *land grabs* came unexpectedly to a head when the major Brazilian daily 'Folha de São Paulo' quoted the president of the Mato Grosso Cotton Producers Association, who claimed that Agriculture Minister José Pacheco had offered 6 m ha of land, without environmental restrictions, free to Brazilian farmers when he visited Brazil on 27 April. This triggered headlines across the world, as well as an angry response from the government. It denied that it would sell land. Brazil could invest, but must create jobs and follow Mozambican regulations. The Council of Ministers had earlier imposed a temporary ban on new land concessions of over 1,000 ha. The local media outcry triggered a strong response from Guebuza; on 22 August he said Mozambicans' conquest of their land must be preserved and that the land law must be scrupulously followed, including with regard to deals between powerful agents. This was clearly aimed at Frelimo party people who had used their positions to obtain land, as well as those who promoted foreign investment.

Meanwhile, existing European investors came into *conflict with local communities* in several parts of the country. The pressure for high profits had pushed foreign companies into seizing land, displacing farmers and threatening their livelihoods and food security. The government accused the Global Solidarity Forest Fund (GSFF), which involves Nordic churches and a major Dutch teachers pension fund, of occupying thousands of hectares of land it had not been allocated, while peasants said they had been pushed off land, and responded by burning forests and chopping down trees. GSFF was forced to replace its entire management in Sweden and Mozambique during the year. Another confrontation was between a Portuguese company, Quifel, a local small soya bean producer backed by the Cooperative League of the USA (Clusa), and the Bill and Melinda Gates Foundation. In 2009, Quifel had told would-be investors it had 30,000 ha for soya in Mozambique, when in practice it apparently had none. In the last concessions before the land freeze, Quifel was given 10,000 ha, but the land included 490 ha occupied by 244 farmers, who had a right to be there as they had occupied the land for more than ten years. Quifel mainly took over a small amount of land already used by the peasant farmers and thus already cleared. By year's end it was still using only a small amount of land, and had never identified the other 20,000 ha it claimed it had been granted. Because land concessions must be put into production within two years, a further confrontation might be expected. But Quifel is well connected; it is controlled by Miguel Pais do Amaral, a Portuguese aristocrat and racing car driver, and Quifel also owns LeYa, which in turn owns two of the most important publishers in Mozambique, Texto Editores and Ndjira, which have published books by local politicians, such as the recent memoires of former president Joaquin Chissano. The land concession freeze was ended in October, and in the final three months of the year five companies were given 330,000 ha – all for trees except for 20,000 ha for sugar and cotton. Meanwhile, SAPPI (originally South African Pulp and Paper Industries), decided not to go ahead with a 150,000 ha eucalyptus plantation in Zambézia province. SAPPI noted that the areas targeted for plantation development had high agricultural potential. They were therefore densely populated, and current land use clearly showed that they were important areas, both at a local and national level, for food production. As a result, any plantation development (own operations and out-grower) would be in direct conflict with agriculture. Trees could only be grown profitably on good farmland which has other potential agricultural uses, and this would lead to conflict with local communities.

China became Mozambique's 10th largest investor, with 7% of FDI in 2010. Chinese companies became increasingly involved in the manufacturing sector, including two cement plants and a cotton gin. China did not have any major involvement in agriculture or mining, although it had been given a heavy sands exploration licence. Illegal shipments of hardwoods continued, organised largely by Chinese businessmen. In July, 561 containers loaded with $ 2 m in valuable timber was stopped at Nacala port;

another 1,000 containers of illegal logs were seized elsewhere. There were complaints that government officials were bribed, but government was cracking down. In September, the provincial director of customs in Nampula (which includes Nacala) was sacked. Agriculture Minister Jose Pacheco told parliament on 17 November that more inspectors had been hired, and that 16 Mozambican and foreign companies (including several owned by Chinese citizens) involved in the illegal export of logs and ivory had had their licences cancelled.

Socioeconomic Developments

Tete province has the world's largest known unexploited reserve of high quality *metallurgical (coking) coal*, and exports of thermal and coking coal were predicted to reach 10 m tonnes in 2013 and 100 m tonnes per year by the end of the decade. Coal mining and exports finally started with the first two mines owned by the Brazilian mining giant Vale and Rio Tinto, which bought the Australian mining company Riversdale. More than 30 mining companies were operating in Tete, mostly developing coal mines, but also iron, vanadium, titanium and rare earths. The Indian company, Jindal Steel and Power, expected to produce 6.6 m tonnes of coal per year. A key problem was transport of the coal to port. The newly upgraded railway to Beira can only carry 6 m tonnes per year and even with further upgrading could only handle 12 m t/y. Vale announced its decision to build a new railway to the much better deep-water port of Nacala. This would involve 60 km of new track in Tete, a 137 km new railway across Malawi (for which agreement was announced on 28 December), and a major rebuilding of the existing 650 km railway to Nacala port. The project would take three years and cost $ 3 bn. The northern

Mozambique railway line and Malawi railways were operated by a company controlled by Vale, with minority shares owned by a Mozambican consortium headed by Insitec.

Plans were made for three large coalfired *power stations* to be built in Tete. The two big coalmining companies, Vale and Riversdale-Rio Tinto, each planned 2,000 MW plants, and on 3 October, the government authorised Jindal Steel and Power to build a 2,640 MW plant. The main market for the electricity would be South Africa. Meanwhile the Rovuma basin, offshore to the north of Mozambique, was proving to be one of the biggest *gas* fields in Africa. During the year, just one US company, Anadarko, raised its estimate of gas reserves from 10 trillion cubic feet to 30 trillion, and was proposing a plant to produce Liquefied Natural Gas that could process a billion cubic feet of gas a day. The Italian company ENI declared there were 22 trillion cubic feet in its block. Total investments could exceed $ 20 bn. There were no finds of commercial quantities of oil, but there were reports that Niassa province, inland near Lake Malawi, had reserves of high quality coal at least as important as those in Tete, as well as substantial reserves of gas.

A new law was introduced which required that by 2012 petrol must contain 10% ethanol and diesel 3% *biodiesel*. There had been rapid expansion of sugar production, partly for ethanol. But the production of jatropha for biodiesel was proving much more difficult. Originally billed as a miracle crop, which was pest resistant and grew on poor soils, it turned out to be productive only on good soils, where it competed with food crops and had serious pest problems. The most advanced foreign investor, the British company Sun Biofuels, went bankrupt in August, and there was no large-scale production of biodiesel from jatropha. One programme, run by a Portuguese consortium headed by GALP, had the first outgrower scheme, involving 300 small farmers growing jatropha.

The *IMF*, in a report of 24 May published on 27 June, said Mozambique's economic growth had not been as pro-poor as in other countries with comparable high and sustainable growth episodes. It had become less pro-poor over time. It also said that "poverty reduction did not reach the magnitude observed in other high-growth countries", and cited the "sharp contrasts" with China, Vietnam, Brazil "and even Uganda". Expenditure declined for the bottom 30% of the population – the poorest were getting poorer. The report warned that, "as income inequality rises, so does the risk of social conflict – as recent events in the Middle East provide a topical reminder of". Mozambique should put more emphasis on economic diversification, the IMF continued. The stagnation in income poverty reduction and the unrest in September 2010 were clear warning signals that the growth model needed complementation by well-targeted efforts to broaden the country's productive and export base and create employment opportunities. Mozambique needed to "diversify its economy away from capital-intensive, low-valued added products" and should "increase production and productivity in labour-intensive sectors, particularly in agriculture". And, in a total reversal of past World Bank and IMF agriculture policy, an IMF staff report called for "subsidized credit in the form of credit guarantees" and "the provision of public goods such as basic research, infrastructure, and agricultural extension services".

The 2009/10 agriculture census, published on 22 November, showed Mozambique to have the lowest *agricultural productivity* in southern Africa. There were 3.8 m farms in the country, but the average farm was only 1.5 ha. Only 4% of farmers used fertiliser and most of those were tobacco farmers in Tete; only 2% were able to obtain credit, and more than one-third of those were Tete tobacco farmers receiving inputs on credit. Only 3% of farmers used pesticides and only 5% used irrigation. Of all farms, 42%

did not produce enough food to feed the farmer's family properly. Major policy shifts were set out in the *Strategic Agriculture Plan* 2011–2020 (PEDSA) approved by the Council of Ministers on 3 May. Donors and foreign investors received hardly a mention; the emphasis was on domestic investment and the development of small and medium commercial farms, making them more productive and competitive. The strategy gave a much more interventionist role to government, explicitly reversing the disastrous farm policies of the World Bank, IMF and donors over the past two decades. There was to be a major expansion of rural extension and agronomic research, both blocked by the World Bank in the past. Priority for state intervention would be input production and supply (including local production and bulk imports of fertilisers), provision of technology packages, animal traction and mechanisation, increased use of water and electricity, and agro-processing. Government would also intervene to ensure seasonal credit for farmers and credit for traders and suppliers, and the provision of insurance, and there would be an expansion of contract farming. The World Bank had also forced the run-down of the *marketing board*, the Mozambique Cereals Institute (Instituto de Cereais de Moçambique – ICM), but the Council of Ministers decided on 28 June that the ICM would return to its traditional role as buyer of last resort, promising to purchase all grain that private traders failed to buy. Agriculture Minister Jose Pacheco declared that one could not risk that farmers increased productivity and output without guaranteeing a market for their surplus.

Another World Bank imposition bit the dust in May, when the state railways company Caminhos de Ferro de Moçambique (CFM) resumed training of permanent way (railway line) maintenance staff. The World Bank had forced privatisation of *railway maintenance* and the dismissal of all the experienced staff who had previously done this work. Other reversals of World Bank policy included the decision not to privatise the state-owned mobile telephone company, mCel, and a decision to open a state-owned grain processing factory in Tete.

A contract was signed in April between the Mozambican government and the Brazilian Development Bank (BNDES) to convert the Nacala military air base into a *commercial airport* with the capacity to handle between 500,000 and 600,000 passengers a year, to promote tourism to northern beaches. The Mozambican government already provided $ 40 m, with the total cost estimated at $ 120 m. Work was to be carried out by the Brazilian company Odebrecht.

After the 1–2 September 2010 riots in Maputo, the government had provided bread subsidies, which in March were announced to be replaced by a subsidised food basket and a subsidised bus pass. By June, however, the government denied that any such thing had been promised, and the ideas were dropped. One reason was action by the Bank of Mozambique to reduce the *exchange rate*. Most food in Maputo is imported from South Africa and in the first half of 2010 the exchange rate had risen from 3.5 to 5 Mozambican Meticais to the South African Rand, causing a major increase in the price of imports, which led to the riots. By the end of 2011, the exchange rate had been pushed back to 3.25 Meticais to the Rand. However, the low exchange rate made it impossible for local producers to compete with imported vegetables.

Minimum wages were raised substantially in April to a minimum for agricultural work of $ 65 per month, a minimum for civil servants of $ 77 and minimum levels in other sectors of $ 90–$ 105 (with one exception – the financial services minimum of $ 173 per month). A study published by the Washington-based Center for Global Development found that there had been a real deterioration of *welfare* in terms of income, food consumption and nutritional status between 2007 and 2008. Meanwhile, a study by KPMG found that Mozambican banks made a profit of $ 143 m in 2009.

The Insitec group became the largest business group, with interests in the second largest bank (BCI), the northern railway and port system, and the company that had the concession for the proposed Mpanda Nkuwa dam (for which the $ 2.4 bn funding was still to be raised). In June, it bought Mozambique's largest building and engineering company, CETA.

In one of the most high-level *corruption* cases, the president of the Constitutional Council (Supreme Court), Luis Mondlane, resigned in disgrace on 17 March after the exposure of his misuse of nearly $ 1 m and his improper dismissal of a court official who had objected. The new president was the highly respected Hemenegildo Gamito. Former transport and communications minister Antonio Munguambe was finally jailed for his part in a $ 3 m corruption case, after his sentence was reduced to four years. On 20 June, Attorney-General Augusto Paulino warned that *organised crime* was directing its profits to real estate. He noted that the Mozambican economy was too small for buildings of the size constructed in the major cities, particularly in the capital. Some of the hotel and private mansions appeared to be funded by drug money.

A revised *budget* was approved by parliament in June. The $ 5 bn budget was financed to 56% by taxes and other state revenue, 42% by aid, and 2% by domestic debt.

Deputy Education Minister Leda Hugo said that the number of higher *education* institutions had increased from 11 in 2000 to 38 in 2010 and the number of students on degree courses increased from 13,200 to 82,000. She also warned about substandard higher education institutions and courses. Eduardo Mondlane University (UEM) was to revert to its previous academic curriculum. The previous rector (vice-chancellor), Filipe

Couto had decided to shorten four-year undergraduate courses to three years to fit in with the Bologna international standard of three years, and reduce medical training from seven years to six. Couto's deputy, Orlando Quilambo, became rector in May, and in October announced the return to the former curriculum because the Bologna model was not viable for UEM. Maria Celeste Onions, Education Ministry head of human resources, said in October that the pupil/teacher ratio in first level primary education (first to fifth grades) was falling slowly, from one teacher per 71 pupils in 2008 to 67 in 2009 and to 66 in 2010. Of the 147,000 employees of the Ministry of Education, including teaching and non-teaching staff, at least 2,216 had died as a result of HIV/AIDS over the previous three years, and 1,999 were living with the HIV virus, of whom 1,738 were taking antiretroviral drugs (ARVs).

Health Minister Alexandre Manguele reported on 26 April that *malaria* remained the main cause of death, despite a reduction in the number of cases. In 2010, the country registered about 3.3 m cases of malaria, a 21% reduction compared with 2009. Deaths fell 25%. Manguele promised that mass distribution of mosquito nets in the provinces would soon start, prioritising areas that had not benefitted from spraying. Mine clearance was still not complete, and mines from three wars continued to kill. It was reported that land mine explosions had killed seven people and maimed a further 24 in 2010. UNDP estimated it would cost $ 21 m to complete mine clearance.

There was a series of kidnappings of at least 15 members of the Asian-Mozambique community and ransoms of up to $ 2 m were demanded. It was believed that members of the Asian community were involved in the kidnappings. Wild animals killed 86 people, and injured a further 60, according to government spokesperson Deputy Justice Minister Alberto Nkutumula. Over 20 elderly people were killed because they were accused of being witches.

Mozambique in 2012

Mozambique is only just adapting to its unexpected future as one of the top ten coal producers and top 20 gas producers in the world by the end of the decade. The government started learning to handle giant multinational mining and petroleum companies. Money would not flow soon, so Mozambique remained aid dependent, but the government made decisions that donors and the World Bank had previously blocked. There was increased jockeying for position as 2014 national elections approached with no clear presidential candidate.

Domestic Politics

The constitution barred President Armando Guebuza from standing for a third term in the 2014 elections. The Frelimo party remained more powerful than any individual and informally rejected soundings by the Guebuza camp to change the constitution as part of *initiatives to retain power for Guebuza*. President of the party and president of the country were separate posts, so it was agreed that Guebuza could retain the powerful post of party president. Frelimo rules gave substantial power to the Political Commission, even over the choice of government. 'O Pais' (28 August) quoted party Secretary-General Filipe Paunde as saying that the party directed the government and the Political Commission instructed the president. Thus Guebuza would remain in a powerful position, but if the national presidential candidate was not a close ally of Guebuza, there could be substantial tension and conflict. So his next move was to promote a weak candidate as next president and he pushed Prime Minister Aires Ali.

 | DOI 10.1163/9789004301122_010

A new party central committee was elected at the 10th Frelimo Congress in Pemba on 23–28 September, and the central committee in turn elected the Political Commission, which ran the party. The central committee would also select the Frelimo candidate for the 2014 *presidential election*. Aires Ali failed to be elected to the Political Commission, and it was unlikely that the Central Committee would choose someone as presidential candidate who had failed to be elected to the Political Commission. Two weeks later, Guebuza dismissed Ali from the post of prime minister. Alberto Vaquina, a medical doctor and governor of Tete and a member of the Political Commission was appointed in his place. Former prime minister and former finance minister Luisa Diogo, who had become the anyone-but-Ali candidate, failed to be re-elected to the Political Commission. So, at the end of the year, there was no obvious presidential candidate. But the Congress underlined that Frelimo remained a democratic and unpredictable party; Guebuza was perhaps powerful, but he did not have absolute control.

The Congress also showed that Frelimo was no longer the party of the workers and peasants, but the party of the bureaucracy: 1,607 of the 1,955 *congress delegates* stated their occupations and 924 (57%) worked for the state or party (108 teachers, 26 nurses, 468 other civil servants, and 322 Frelimo staff). Only 126 delegates (8%) were farmers, seven (0.4%) were industrial workers and 289 (18%) were technicians, while 129 (8%) described themselves as business people or proprietors.

The main *opposition party*, Renamo, became increasingly marginal. On 8 March, there was a shootout between Renamo and the police; one policeman was killed and 23 Renamo people were arrested. In October, party leader Dhlakama and some of his supporters moved to rural Gorongosa district in central Mozambique, threatening to destroy the country if the government did not meet his demands. On 23 October, he demanded that Guebuza come to Gorongosa to see him to negotiate a transitional government. Three rounds of inconclusive talks were held in Maputo in December between a government delegation headed by Agriculture Minister Jose Pacheco, who was a member of the Frelimo Political Commission, and a Renamo delegation headed by the party's new Secretary General Manuel Bissopo. On 18 April, a *by-election* in Inhambane caused by the death of the mayor was won by Frelimo's Benedito Guimino with 78% of the votes, on a respectable 39% turnout. The Mozambique Democratic Movement (MDM) received 22% and Renamo boycotted the election.

New *election laws* were agreed by parliament in December. Municipal elections would be held in November 2013 and national elections, for president, national parliament, and provincial parliaments, in October 2014. There would be a new registration in 2013 and an update in 2014. The new elections commission would have eight members in proportion to parliamentary representation (five Frelimo, two Renamo, one MDM), one judge, one prosecutor, and three members of civil society organisations. The law was agreed very late, in part because of the agreement between donors and government to end the donor strike (see Foreign Affairs). After confusion and incompetence during the 2009 elections, both the Constitutional Council (the highest court) and civil society organisations called for a unified electoral code rather than a set of different and contradictory laws. This would be drawn up outside parliament to avoid traditional party battles and Renamo intransigence. But the one concession that the government made to donors was to accept the somewhat unusual donor demand that civil society organisations and the Constitutional Council be ignored, and the old package of laws simply be amended.

Parliament approved a strong *Public Probity Law* on 11 May. The approval confounded sceptics, who were convinced that parliamentary leaders would not vote to cut their own incomes. The law created a category of office holders including the president, ministers, members of parliament, presidents of provincial and municipal assemblies, *vereadores* (municipal ministers), and district administrators, all subject to special restrictions: They were barred from receiving any other income from the state or from state companies; office holders and their close relatives could not enter into any type of contract with the state or state companies. The law was controversial because many parliamentary leaders also had well paid posts as directors of state companies, which they would be forced to give up, although they had not done so by the end of 2012. The new law defined a public servant as anyone in a public entity. The definition was very broad, covering office holders as well as members of provincial and municipal assemblies, normal civil servants at both national and municipal level, the military and police, and even employees of private contractors carrying out public functions. The law barred public servants from using their power or influence to provide any special help to themselves, their family, friends or anyone else – whether or not they were being paid for the help – and imposed restrictions on earning outside income. All public servants were now required to file annual asset and income declarations, and there would be a public register listing declarations made, although the declarations themselves would be secret and there were heavy penalties for publishing information from them, so they could not be checked by the public.

The core political problem was on-going *poverty*. Mozambique was a country with a high growth rate but it failed to convert growth into poverty reduction. A report issued on 11 May by the Africa Progress Panel, chaired by Kofi Annan, noted that Mozambique was one of the more unequal countries, with the top 10% of the population having an income 19 times that of the poorest 10%. The report cited Mozambique as the fifth fastest growing country in Africa, but pointed out that household survey evidence showed no decrease in national poverty and a marked increase in poverty in the central regions. It noted that Mozambique was a net importer of staple foods and that above 70% of working youth lived on less than $ 1.25 a day. Catholic bishops issued a statement after their 6–13 November conference that the poor were increasingly poor. The gains from natural resources were not contributing to the improvement of conditions for ordinary people. According to the World Bank 2013 World Development Report, published on 1 October, agricultural productivity and rural living standards had not improved. Productivity was low because of extremely rudimentary technologies. People did not migrate because there were no jobs to move to. The report also warned that social discontent appeared to be on the rise. In June, IMF Deputy Director for Africa Roger Nord referred in London to Mozambique as a country where the poor had benefited less from growth, and warned that this could raise social tension. An article in 'World Development' diagnosed households in rural Mozambique as "collectively trapped in generalised underdevelopment" with relative stagnation. Some speakers at the Frelimo 10th Congress on 23–28 September were also critical. Zacarias Kupela, former head of the Frelimo youth movement, pointed to the widening gap between rich and poor and warned that "future generations will reap the whirlwinds and cyclones". Graça Machel criticised self-serving party members who satisfied their egotistic, corrupt, ambitious and opportunist interest. Former president Luiz Lula of Brazil gave a talk on 19 November in Maputo, in which he warned against leaders who sought a third term. In another speech to local businesspeople he said, "No Mozambican can feel proud to open their car door and see a hungry person looking for something to eat in the rubbish." President Guebuza attacked his critics on 6 December in an extemporaneous speech to the congress of the Mozambique Workers Organisation ('Organização dos Trabalhadores de Moçambique'). According to the government daily 'Noticias' (23 November), Guebuza criticised "professional agitators acting in bad faith, and in the name of friendship with the poor [who are] alleging that only some people are benefitting from natural resources and from wealth". Some foreigners "come here and say the gap between the rich and poor is increasing". Speaking in Xai-Xai on 10 November, he said, "Only the lazy believe we cannot end poverty." Minimum wages were raised to $ 83 per month for agricultural workers and $ 90–$ 130 per month in most other sectors.

For ordinary people, the cost of living, unemployment and inflation were the three most serious problems, according to a secret *government survey*. The survey, carried out for government by a private agency in 2010 but never published, was leaked and posted on the website of the Public Integrity Centre. It listed corruption as only the seventh most serious issue, although, 74% of families considered corruption to be serious or very serious. More than half (52%) of the families interviewed admitted to paying bribes in order to obtain basic public services. Only 10% had used the court system, but half of those admitted paying bribes. Payment of bribes was most frequent in education (23%) and health (22%). The media scored very high marks for integrity.

Foreign Affairs

Mozambique was once one of the most aid-dependent countries in the world. The discovery of huge resources and the potential income in mineral and hydrocarbon revenues in a few years time was already changing both *government and donor attitudes*.

Donors and the international financial institutions, the World Bank and IMF, had previously dominated policy formation in a quite brazen way. Donors remained anxious to continue to spend in Mozambique, but they began switching money away from general budget support to support for specific projects and ministries, where they could exercise more leverage. Meanwhile, the government announced the reversal of two donor-imposed policies. In December, ignoring earlier interventions by donors, the government bought the remaining shares in Banco Nacional de Investimento to make it into a development bank and the agricultural marketing board was re-established. Two government-owned grain mills opened. A particular confrontation was with the United States Millennium Challenge Corporation (MCC), which had signed a five-year $507 m agreement in 2007. The MCC made extension of the contract conditional on a form of land privatisation, but the government refused and the contract was not renewed.

US President Barack Obama announced in Washington on 18 May that Mozambique had been chosen as one of six countries to benefit from a G8 programme to use the private sector to end hunger. The New Alliance for Food Security and Nutrition project used aid money to subsidise giant *agribusinesses* to take over large tracts of land. A similar programme called ProSavana was also launched, which involved Japanese aid to support Brazilian agribusinesses to take large tracts for soya production. Neither moved forward, however, because of the difficulty of accumulating large tracts of land. Under Mozambican law, occupiers had rights to the land and could not be moved for farming without agreement (although they could be moved for mines). The National Peasants Union ('União Nacional de Camponeses') issued a statement on 11 October in which it strongly condemned ProSavana as a top-down project being run in secret, which would make peasants landless and impoverish rural communities.

The death of *Malawi* president Bingu wa Mutharika in April and his replacement by Joyce Banda allowed the neighbours to repair relations. Banda visited Mozambique on 13–15 May. Mozambican President Armando Guebuza took over as *chair of SADC* in early August, and one of his first tasks was to meet Rwanda's President Paul Kagame in Kigali (Rwanda) on 28 August to deliver a message from the SADC heads of state summit in Maputo on 17–18 August, which accused Rwanda of interfering in the DRC by supporting the M23 rebels. The response came on 12 October, when Rwandan opposition figure and former director of the Rwandan Development Bank, Theogene Turatsinze. was murdered in Maputo. Speaking on behalf of SADC in October at the EU headquarters in Brussels (Belgium), Gubueza demanded that the deadline for signing the controversial *EPAs* should be extended from the end of 2014 for two years until 2016, to allow more time for negotiations. Guebuza also became head of the *CPLP* at a meeting in Maputo on 20 July. The CPLP continued to recognise Raimundo Pereira as president of Guinea Bissau, despite his overthrow by the military, and Guebuza again demanded Pereira's return. Former Mozambique president Joaquin Chissano had been SADC mediator on *Madagascar* since 2009 when Andry Rajoelina took over with military backing, but had failed to resolve the issue. An unsuccessful meeting with Rajoelina took place in Dar es Salaam (Tanzania) in December, when Chissano and Tanzanian President Jakaya Kikwete unsuccessfully urged Rajoelina not to stand in the next presidential elections.

Socioeconomic Developments

Huge discoveries of coal and gas reserves resulted in a resource frenzy. More than $ 2.7 bn was already invested in exploration activities. The existence of *gas* along the coast of southern Inhambane province had been known since the 1960s. A pipeline had been built and the South African petrochemical company Sasol had been importing gas since 2004. But explorations off shore in the north of the country, on the border with Tanzania, discovered a huge gas reserve (although no oil), estimated at 100 trillion ft^3, worth an estimated $ 350 bn, from which Mozambique could hope to earn at least $ 1 bn per year from royalties alone, plus company profits and taxes. The government owned between 10% and 25% of all gas projects through Empresa Nacional de Hidrocarbonetos, the state oil and gas company. Gas would be liquefied and exported. Anadarko of the USA and ENI of Italy agreed to build a joint gas liquefaction plant that would be the second largest in the world (after Qatar), at an estimated cost of an incredible $ 50 bn. The reserves were the third largest in Africa, after Algeria and Nigeria, and exploration continued.

Huge *coal* reserves were discovered in Tete and Niassa provinces. By 2015, Mozambique could produce 100 m tonnes per year (m t/y) of coal, half of it high-quality coking coal, from which the country could earn at least $ 300 m per year in royalties. Two companies began producing and two more expected to start in 2013, but the coal mines were 600 km to 800 km from the sea and the current rail capacity was just 6 m t/y, in part because of the World Bank fiasco with the *Sena railway line*. In a damning evaluation, the World Bank admitted responsibility for the failure to complete upgrading of the line from the Tete coal mines to the port of Beira, which should have been finished in 2009. The $ 110 m World Bank loan was conditional on Mozambique Railways ('Caminhos de Ferro de Moçambique'; CFM) retrenching 13,600 experienced staff, and on the structure of the central railways being a concession in which the concessionaire had 51% of the shares and CFM 49%, which left CFM without influence. The failure of the project was blamed on this Bank-imposed structure. The Bank gave the contract to an Indian Rites and Ircon consortium, which allegedly lacked experience and competence. Repeated and valid complaints by CFM and the government were ignored. Finally, the report admitted that Mozambique not only had to repay the loan for the unsatisfactory project, but also had to find money to complete the work and to pay an extra $ 20 m to the contractor, which was considered unjustified because of ineffective Bank monitoring.

The Brazilian company Vale began building an entirely *new railway line* from its mines in Tete across Malawi and back into Mozambique to the port of Nacala. Rio Tinto proposed a new railway line to a new offshore floating terminal north of Quelimane. A third railway line was also suggested, entirely within Mozambique, from Tete to Nacala, but there would not be adequate export capacity until 2015–17. Meanwhile, the companies were proposing *thermal power stations* in Tete to burn low quality coal not worth exporting and produce 6,400 MW in three power stations. However, South Africa, the most likely buyer of energy, showed no interest. The low-grade coal was therefore likely to pile up for the next few years. Mozambique took over the final 15% of the Cahora Bassa dam under a complex deal agreed on 9 April. Mozambique paid $ 42 m for 7.5% and would trade shares in the proposed central-south power line for the other 7.5%.

Membership in the *Extractive Industries Transparency Initiative* (EITI) was approved on 26 October, after having been rejected once. This meant that all payments by mining companies were now public, although contracts and the way payments were calculated remained secret. Royalties were set at 6% of the sale price for gas and 3% for coal, but the government was to accept company declarations of the sale price. The minerals ministry trained 4,000 people, but their training was largely dependent on the mining and hydrocarbon companies, so there were growing civil society complaints that they would not become independent of the industry.

The *tax authorities* began informal negotiations to fill loopholes. When Cove Energy, which owned 8.5% of one of the gas blocks, was sold to PTT of Thailand for $ 1.9 bn, it was agreed that $ 175 m would be paid to the government. At the end of the year, parliament passed a new tax law, which set a 32% capital gains tax on sales or transfers of mineral or hydrocarbon assets in Mozambique. On 11 December, the government announced for the first time that 2.8% of mineral revenues would be spent in local communities, and that the first $ 1 m would go to communities affected by coal mining in Moatize, Tete, and by heavy sands mining in Moma, Nampula province.

Meanwhile the coal mining companies continued to have *problems with local communities*. On 10 January, more than 500 families blocked the road and railway line in Tete to protest about their resettlement by the Brazilian company Vale from an area that was to become an opencast mine. Riot police were called and 14 people were arrested. But then-governor Alberto Vaquina later admitted that the community's claims were valid – new houses had been badly built and the community had not been given the promised water and agricultural support. Two weeks later, Vale was given the annual Public Eye award for the worst corporate conduct by activists at the World Economic Forum in Davos (Switzerland). Minerals Minister Esperança Bias took the remarkable decision to have a ministry coordinating council meeting in the resettlement village of Cateme in August, with ministry staff staying with families in the resettlement houses. It became clear that the problems that had caused the demonstration in January had not been solved. The government bought 5% of Vale interests for $ 21 m under the original contract, which promised 10% to Mozambican investors.

The IMF declared in a statement on 21 December that Mozambique's *economic performance* was remarkable and that the prudent execution of the budget had contributed to a judicious policy mix that fostered economic stability, despite global uncertainty. Inflation was just 2%, well under the target of 5.6%. The IMF reported that GDP had increased as estimated by 7.5%. FDI was 17% of GDP, compared with 5% in 2009. During the year, the Mozambican metical (MZN) remained stable at MZN 3.5 to the South African rand; this was important to prevent riots, since many key goods in Maputo were imported from South Africa. By contrast, the metical fell 9.7% in relation to the US dollar to MZN 29.6 to $ 1.

Reflecting the low inflation, the base *interest rate* (paid by commercial banks to borrow from the central bank) was cut from 15% to 10.5% by late 2012. Despite the sharp fall in both inflation and central bank interest rates, private banks continued to charge more than 20% interest – double the central bank rate. Mohanad Rafik, chair of the government's Economic Recovery Support Fund (FARE), accused microfinance institutions of usury. He said FARE lent at 8%–12% interest to microfinance institutions but they lent on to rural producers at 30%–60% interest. *Banks* were still regionally concentrated. There were 470 branches of commercial banks, of which 218 were in Maputo city and province. Of the 128 districts in Mozambique, only 58 had banks and there were banks in only three of the 15 districts in Niassa, and four of the 16 districts in the neighbouring province of Cabo Delgado. The picture was even worse with regard to micro-credit. Of the 182 micro-credit operators in the country, 130 were in Maputo city and province.

Other economic activities included two major projects by China in Maputo, a $ 1 bn bridge to Katembe (the part of Maputo on the other side of the bay, currently reached by ferry) and toll road to South Africa, and a $ 315 m ring road around Maputo based on a largely colonial plan. The EU signed a new fisheries agreement, allowing 75 boats to catch 460,000 tonnes per year, mostly of tuna. Biofuel production remained stalled, except for ethanol from sugar, so the government suspended plans to require 10% ethanol in petrol and 3% biofuel in diesel.

Data released for 2011 showed how overstretched the *education system* was, and its low quality. There were nearly 6 m children in school and 109,000 teachers. Of 248,000 people employed in the public sector, 44% were teachers. But in primary school, there were 63 pupils for each teacher. Pass rates were low. Of pupils who entered the fifth (final) year of primary school, only 63% passed – 22% failed and 14% dropped out. Pass rates in secondary school were 64% for tenth grade and 52% for twelfth grade. The Ministry of Education admitted that no well-trained teachers from the Pedagogic University had been hired during the past three years because graduates were too expensive, and that it was cheaper to pay poorly trained teachers for extra sessions.

Other *statistics* showed that Mozambique had one of the higher traffic accident death rates in the world; in the first half of 2012, 730 people were killed on the road. Mozambique had 33 mobile telephones for every 100 people. Kidnappings for ransom continued in the Asian business community. Businessman Momed Ayoob was gunned down on the street on 20 April. In 2010, he had been arrested in Swaziland carrying $ 2.7 m in cash, and had been accused in the Mozambican press of being involved in drug dealing.

Mozambique in 2013

The implication of having one of the world's largest gas fields was dawning on local elites and everyone wanted a share. After 20 years of peace, Renamo launched new attacks on road traffic and the army. Doctors went on strike. The gas field was not yet producing, but $ 624 m in capital gains taxes transformed relations with donors. Meanwhile, governing party Frelimo's main concerns were the succession and opposition successes in local elections.

Domestic Politics

Opposition party *Renamo* unexpectedly resumed *military action*, ending 20 years of peace. Renamo had signed a peace accord with the government in 1992 after a 15-year war and had stood in 1994 multi-party elections, becoming the main opposition party. But with the tacit acceptance of both the government and the international community, it retained small military bases and an armed militia called a "presidential guard". Renamo had held up approval of electoral legislation, demanding the politicisation of the electoral administration and an effective veto over election decisions. When legislation was passed at the last minute, despite Renamo objections, Renamo's leader, Alfonso Dhlakama, announced a boycott of elections, including not taking up Renamo posts on election commissions. Renamo Secretary-General Manuel Bissopo said on 29 March that Renamo was prepared to go to war to prevent registration and elections. In the early morning of 3 April, the riot police (Força de Intervenção Rápida) raided Renamo party headquarters in Muxungué, Sofala province, and Gondola, Manica province. There were hundreds of men in each

 | DOI 10.1163/9789004301122_011

place, including some former guerrillas from the 1977–92 war. Renamo said that the gatherings were legal political meetings, just two of many being held by the party to mobilise against elections. The government called them military training camps. Two days later, Renamo guerrillas attacked a police post in Muxungué, killing four policemen, and the next days attacked traffic on the main north-south N1 road, killing three people.

Talks between the government and Renamo resumed on 2 May. The government delegation was headed by Agriculture Minister José Pacheco, a member of the Frelimo Political Commission. Renamo put four issues on the agenda: revision of the electoral law to give Renamo "parity"; reversal of the marginalisation of Renamo in the military; equitable distribution of wealth and greater participation by Renamo members in the economy; and reversal of the partyisation of the civil service. The second and third issues had long histories. When the peace accord was signed in 1992, Mozambique was a poor country with no mineral wealth; now with huge gas and coal reserves, there was much more money in circulation, and some elite Frelimo members had become relatively (and ostentatiously) wealthy. Frelimo membership seemed important for contracts, loans, promotions, etc., while known opposition members seemed to be excluded. Thus a key demand was for money, and for a higher status for Dhlakama and the Renamo military leadership. Speaking at a press conference on 10 April in Satunjira, Dhlakama said he had authorised the April attacks only because formers guerrillas said they would kill him if he did not. Local media unofficially confirmed this. Renamo generals felt they had not gained from 20 years of peace and wanted status and money.

Violence resumed on 24 May near Satunjira, when there was a shoot-out between the military and the Renamo presidential guard. On 17 June, Renamo attacked a military post and arms depot at Savana, along the main railway from the Tete coalmines to Beira port. Five government soldiers were killed and arms taken. On 19 June, Renamo announced it would cut road traffic on the main north-south N1 road, on the 100 km between Muxungué and the River Save. This was symbolically important because Renamo guerrillas had killed many people in that section of the road during the 1977–92 war. On 21 June, Renamo attacked road traffic, killing two people. The government reintroduced military convoys along that section of road, and there was a series of further ambushes over the rest of the month, as well as military confrontations near Gorongosa.

The number of incidents decreased and Renamo held a meeting with 300 party militants on 29–31 July in Satunjira. On the first day, Dhlakama made a very strong statement threatening to divide the country in half during the next week. After being contacted by ambassadors from the US and EU, he backed down. Renamo briefed the press that the ambassadors had promised that Frelimo would make concessions, but other sources denied this, and no concessions were offered at the next round of talks. *Fighting resumed* when Renamo attacked a police post in Muanza on 12 October, and there were gunfights between the two sides near Satunjira. On 21 October, the army occupied the Satunjira base. Dhlakama and Bissopo escaped, but Armindo Milaco, an MP and Renamo head of mobilisation, was killed. Dhlakama's whereabouts were not disclosed, but he apparently retreated to another former base in the dense forest further up the mountain. The army moved on to occupy the Renamo base at nearby Maringué, which had remained a Renamo military base since the end of the war in 1992 with the tacit acceptance of the government and local police.

Renamo stopped attending talks with the government and launched *more attacks* on the N1 south of Muxungué and around Gorongosa, and opened new fronts. Former guerrillas occupied a former base in northern Nampula province, and several times attacked the main road near Rapale, killing at least two people. Near the end of the year, guerrilla groups moved into Tete province near the border with Malawi, and into Homoine, Inhambane, which was the site of the worst Renamo massacre during the war. During the year, at least 60 people were killed and more than 300 injured in Renamo attacks and fighting between Renamo and the government.

The UN Special Rapporteur on extreme poverty and human rights, Magdalena Sepulveda, told a Maputo press conference on 16 April that during her visit she had witnessed very high standards of comfort in some areas of Maputo city, which contrasted dramatically with the harsh reality in larger areas of the capital. "If not addressed urgently, such marked *disparities and high levels of social exclusion* may pose a threat to social stability, as foreshadowed by protests in Maputo in recent years", she warned. In partial response, the government pushed the exchange rate with the South African rand below MZN (meticais) 3 to the rand in June, and kept it there for the rest of the year. Riots in the capital Maputo and the adjoining city of Matola in 2008 and 2010 had been partly over the cost of living, and most food and consumer goods in Maputo and Matola were imported from South Africa, so keeping the exchange rate overvalued kept the cost of living down in the capital. But it also meant that local producers could not compete with imported chickens, pigs, tomatoes and other fruit and vegetables. With the metical this low, South Africa goods were cheaper than local products even in places like Chimoio, more than 1,000 km from South Africa.

Demands to spread the wealth became more frequent. The Forum of Demobilised Soldiers had several confrontations with riot police as it attempted to demonstrate in front of the prime minister's office to push its claim for a much higher pension for all demobilised troops. Doctors went on strike in May, complaining that they were paid less than university professors and judges. The strike was mostly supported in Maputo and Nampula, and was abandoned by the doctors in June without gaining any concessions. Participants were penalised and leaders forced to retire. In November, hundreds of former secret police agents, as well as widows and children, demonstrated on 7 November in front of the office of President Armando Guebuza over what they said was the failure to pay their pensions.

There were also increasing reports of teachers and others being forced to donate to Frelimo, and of teachers linked to opposition parties being transferred to remote schools. The *Afrobarometer survey* carried out in late 2012 was published in late 2013. People in 34 African countries had been asked how free they were to say what they thought. A surprisingly high 33% in Mozambique said they were not free, compared with only 7% in Tanzania, 13% in Malawi, and 16% in South Africa – and 53% in Zimbabwe and 57% in Swaziland. Mozambicans were optimistic about the future but rated the government badly on job creation: 47% of Mozambicans felt the government was managing the economy well, but 60% said it was doing badly at improving the standard of living, 65% said it was doing badly at job creation and 63% said it was failing to narrow the gap between rich and poor. And 25% said their living conditions were good, 43% neither good nor bad, and 32% bad – but 68% expected them to improve in the next year.

In mid-2013, Guebuza moved to take tighter control of his party. Leaders of the youth organisation ('Organizacao da Juventude Mocambicana') and women's organisation ('Organizacao das Mulheres Mocambicanas') were replaced by *Guebuza loyalists*. Edson Macuacua, who had been marginalised as Frelimo party press spokesperson after the Frelimo Congress in 2012 when he was sharply criticised for his heavy-handed treatment of the media, was unexpectedly named Guebuza's press spokesman and began a campaign to improve the president's image. Rogério Sitoe, the respected editor of the state-owned daily 'Notícias', was dismissed in August. His replacement was an explicitly political appointment, Jaime Langa, who had no journalistic experience but was a Frelimo *vereador* (local minister) in Matola. Subsequently, the newspaper ran more articles praising Guebuza's achievements, and the main picture on the front page was usually of Guebuza. In September, Jeremias Langa was dismissed as editorial director of 'O Pais', the main independent daily newspaper, and director of information of STV, the main independent television station; both had come under pressure for being too critical of Frelimo.

Frelimo maintained its dominance in the 20 November *municipal elections*, winning the post of mayor and a majority in the municipal assembly in 49 of 53 municipalities. But the opposition Mozambique Democratic Movement (MDM) made its mark, winning three important cities – Nampula, Quelimane and Beira – and 30% of assembly seats nationally. In Maputo and Matola, the MDM won 40% and 42% of the vote, respectively, compared with Renamo's 14% and 9% in the previous local elections in 2008. Renamo boycotted the election but, despite threats, did not try to disrupt registration or the election. The results confirmed the MDM as the main opposition party. Turnout was 46%, the same as in 2008, but above the 28% of 2003. Registration from 25 May to 23 June hit 85% of the estimated number of voting age adults (who would be 18 years old on 20 November) in the 53 municipalities, which have about one quarter of the Mozambican population. (Mozambique remains predominantly rural, and government structures in rural areas are appointed by central government.) The Constitutional Council threw out the results in one city, Gurué, because of corruption within the electoral administration, and forced a rerun, scheduled for 8 February 2014.

A short list of three *presidential candidates* for the national election due on 15 October 2014 was announced by the Frelimo Political Commission on 11 December. The final choice was to be made by a meeting of the party's Central Committee in 2014. The three candidates, all technicians from the centre and north and aged between 55 and 58, were: Agriculture Minister José Pacheco, a member of the Frelimo Political Commission and secretary of its Verification Committee; Prime Minister Alberto Vaquina, also a member of the Political Commission; and Defence Minister Filipe Nyusi, the only candidate to have a liberation war link, having attended the Frelimo school in Tunduru (Tanzania), before independence.

Foreign Affairs

A totally unexpected government-guaranteed $ 850 m European *bond issue* on 5 September raised funds for six coastal patrol boats and 24 tuna fishing boats for a new Mozambican government fishing company, Ematum (National Tuna Company), part-owned by the security services. Within Mozambique, there had been no internal discussion, no parliamentary approval, and even many ministers did not know about the bond issue or the new company. The bond was oversubscribed and increased, because it was government backed and at above-average interest rates. An IMF mission at the end of October was very angry with the bond issue and the final IMF statement was quite strong, saying the bond issue should "be included in the 2014 budget and transparently reflected in the fiscal accounts". Budget support donors were appalled, and several delayed disbursements. The government eventually agreed to include $ 350 m of the bond revenue, the amount allocated for military equipment, in the state budget.

The bond issue reflected a rapid change in *donor-government relations*. For more than two decades, Mozambique had been heavily donor dependent, which gave donors much more power than they had in many other African countries. Indeed, by 2009 the G-19 group of 19 budget support donors had become the main forum for dialogue on government policy. But at the same time, the very large investments in coal and gas were coming on stream, along with the realisation that within five years donor funds would be less important. The government began to resist what it saw as donor arrogance. A group of budget support donors had withheld aid for three months at the start of 2010 to put pressure on what they saw as 'governance' improvement. The government had resisted, and donors relented. Since then donors had reduced budget support and moved aid to support projects and individual ministries, where they felt they could wield more power. Foreign aid paid 51% of the state budget in 2010 but only 34% in 2013. On the other hand, donor support for civil society had increased, as had open support, especially from the USA, for openly anti-Frelimo groups. Donors again withheld budget support over Ematum, but the government made few concessions. This marked the *end of donor power*. The US Millennium Challenge Corporation (MCC) refused to grant a second aid package to Mozambique, surprising government ministers, who said they had expected a renewal. The MCC gave no reasons, but three factors seemed important: the Ematum bond further soured relations with the US, several MCC projects had not been completed on time, and Mozambique was refusing to agree to land privatisation, which had been a condition of the first compact. On 24 July, President Guebuza visited the Scottish oil city of Aberdeen, where he was trying to develop alternative *British support* for the oil and gas sector.

Guebuza completed his term as chair of *SADC* on 18 August and former finance minister Tomas Salomão stepped down as

SADC executive secretary after two four-year terms. Mozambique turned down an opportunity to take the *AU* vice presidency from southern Africa for 2014 and thus become chair in 2015, giving the post to Zimbabwe which was next in line, so Robert Mugabe would be AU chair in 2015. The AU chair takes office in January, which is when the new Mozambican president, to be elected in October 2014, would be sworn in, and it seemed inappropriate for a new president to immediately become AU chair.

Relations with neighbouring *Malawi* had improved greatly since Joyce Banda became Malawi's president. In April, Guebuza visited Malawi and signed an agreement for a power interconnection to allow the sale of electricity to Malawi; the agreement had been blocked by the previous president, Bingu wa Mutharika.

Socioeconomic Developments

2013 saw the worst *floods* since 2000. In January, the Limpopo River flooded. The town of Chokwé was completely under water and the government provided humanitarian assistance to 172,000 people in 62 accommodation centres. There was also major damage to irrigation systems along the river. In September, the government admitted that of 285,000 people forced to move after the 2007 floods, the government had so far resettled only 163,000.

Minimum wages, negotiated annually, were announced in April, and remained unchanged at $ 83 per month in agriculture, $ 131 in manufacturing, and $ 90 in public administration. There had been large increases in 2011 and 2012.

In July and August, panic hit the suburbs of Matola and Maputo with people believing that there was a *crime* wave being committed by an organised group called G-20 (group of 20), which attacked with gratuitous violence, including using a hot clothes iron to burn people's arms. A photograph of a woman burned with an iron was circulated on mobile phones. Many people were afraid to sleep in their houses at night and many neighbourhoods set up community patrols and vigilante groups, who caught some thieves. The suburbs had high crime rates and were vulnerable because there were few lights and no police, and houses could be easily broken into. In fact, G-20 did not exist, no one ever complained to the police of being attacked with a hot iron, and the infamous photograph, taken from the Internet, was actually of a Brazilian woman who had been attacked by her ex-husband. The fact that the rumour was believed, and the resulting panic, indicated the widespread lack of confidence in the ability of the government and the police to protect people.

The wave of *kidnappings* for ransom continued, with 44 cases in 2013 – 31 in Maputo, nine in Matola, three in Beira and one in Nampula; there were 20 prosecutions of alleged kidnappers, leading to some convictions. Three policemen (including a member of the elite presidential guard) and three others were each sentenced to 16 years in jail for kidnapping six people in 2011 and 2012. It was revealed in court that ransoms of $ 165,000, $ 160,000, and $ 130,000 had been paid for three kidnap victims. The Confederation of Mozambican Business Associations referred in a statement on 7 November to "the climate of *tension and insecurity* generated by two phenomena that are happening at the same time – the attacks on civilian vehicles in the central zone, and the kidnappings in the major urban areas". Some Mozambicans of Asian origin and some Portuguese business people temporarily left the country, or at least sent their families away. At the peak of the crisis, in late October and early November, regular Council of Ministers meetings were cancelled.

ProSavana, one of Mozambique's largest development projects, became a hot potato. This joint Japanese-Brazilian programme in

Nampula province, upper Zambézia, and western Niassa, initially based on a Japanese-funded programme in the Brazilian *cerrado* (savanna) in the 1970s, was opening up the area for very large corporate soya farms. ProSavana was very donor-driven and was specifically aimed at encouraging Brazilian companies to open giant farms in this area. However, objections from both local communities and the Mozambican Ministry of Agriculture led to major changes, including paying more attention to support for local farmers. On 8 August, Agriculture Minister José Pacheco attended a meeting between civil society representatives and stakeholders of Japan, Brazil and Mozambique, organised through two Mozambican peasant organisations. It revealed major divisions. On the one hand, the ProSavana office produced a draft plan saying that one of the highest priorities was to promote large-scale investment. On the other, National Director of Economy in the Ministry of Agriculture Raimundo Matule told the meeting that, while the target of the Brazilian *cerrado* programme was to promote big industrial agriculture, the target in Mozambique was to support tiny, small and medium farms.

Mozambique has exploitable *gas reserves* of more than 170 trillion ft^3 and more than $ 25 bn was being invested to construct liquefied natural gas production facilities, which could be second largest after Qatar. Exports would not begin until 2019 but large amounts of revenue were already coming in from capital gains tax on the sales of parts of the reserves by the original exploration companies, Anadarko of the US and ENI of Italy. Interest was largely from Asia, which wanted assured gas supplies, and parts continued to be sold to Chinese, Thai, Korean and Indian companies. The IMF estimated that capital gains tax payments amounted to $ 624 m, 4% of GDP. Production of small amounts of *crude oil* began in an area linked to gas fields in Inhambane province; there was no evidence of oil anywhere else in Mozambique.

Mozambique has the fifth largest *coking coal reserves* in the world, and exports had begun. Two problems for the coal mining companies had been transport of the coal to seaports and the poor quality coal lying on top of the coking coal, which must be removed, but is not worth exporting. Up to an estimated 100 m tonnes of coal per year could be exported, but the only *railway* connection, the 578-km Sena line to Beira port, could only carry 6.5 m tonnes. This railway was being expanded and would carry 15 m tonnes a year from 2015. The Brazilian mining giant Vale was upgrading and constructing a 912-km railway line to Nacala port, the longest of the railway lines, including upgrading existing lines and adding 136 km of new railway in Malawi, It would open in late 2014 and would be able to carry 18 m tonnes a year by 2017. A third and totally new railway would follow the shortest route, 525 km, and take coal to a new offshore port at Macuze, just north of Quelimane. It had been the subject of controversy, because the Council of Ministers said the contract would go to the Frelimo-owned company SPI. Transport Minister Paulo Zucula went against this and put the contract out to tender, but this was cancelled by Prime Minister Alberto Vaquina. The prime minister of Thailand visited Mozambique in July and it was announced that the contract would be given, without tender, to Thai Moçambique Logistica, 60% owned by the Italian-Thai Development Company, 20% by the Mozambican state railway company CFM, and 20% by a new Zambezia Integrated Development Corridor company. Zucula was dismissed, and the contract was signed on 13 December. Construction would not start until 2016 and would take five years.

All of the Tete coalmines depend for their profitability on using the poorest quality thermal coal on site in coal-fired *power stations*. South Africa's Eskom had been the obvious customer for the electricity generated because it had been short of power in recent years, but had declined to buy any more electricity from

Mozambique and was instead building two giant coal-fired power stations of its own, which when complete in 2018 would give South Africa surplus capacity. However, on 14 October Ncondezi Energy signed a 25-year 'non-binding' agreement with the state-owned Electricidade de Mozambique (EdM) to buy all the electricity from a 300 MW integrated thermal coal mine and power plant. Power generation should begin in 2017. It was announced in August that a 150 MW gas-fired power station, the largest thermal power station so far built in the country, would be installed at Ressano Garcia, on the border between Mozambique and South Africa, in a partnership between EdM (51%) and the South African Sasol New Energy (49%) It was estimated to cost $ 250 m and should come on stream in 2014. The gas would come from the Inhambane gas fields.

A Mozambican *anti-corruption* NGO, the Centre for Public Integrity (CIP), reported in November that, although Mozambique had been exporting natural gas by pipeline to South Africa since 2004, the revenue earned by the Mozambican state from this activity was insignificant. CIP calculated that gas worth more than $ 700 m crossed the border annually, but the Mozambican government's take was less than $ 10 m a year. Similarly, according to a study by CIP and the European Network on Debt and Development, published in December, Mozambique was deriving very little benefit from the mining of titanium-bearing heavy mineral sand deposits in the northern province of Nampula, thanks to the excessively favourable terms granted to the operator, the Irish company, Kenmare Resources. Kenmare's deal with the government included "contract secrecy, no corporate taxes for one part of the company group, and a halving of corporate taxes for ten years for the other part, no payment of value added tax for several goods, and no import or export taxes". Kenmare's only asset was the mine in Moma, which operated through a chain of eight companies, mostly registered in Mauritius and the British tax haven of Jersey. On 29 August, the director of the Central Office for the Fight against Corruption, Ana Maria Gemo, announced that it was investigating possible criminal practices at the Administrative Tribunal, the country's highest audit body. An audit showed $ 6 m in possible irregularities, including improper payments to suppliers and the hiring of Tribunal staff themselves as consultants. She also said that 599 cases against members of the public administration were processed by her office between January and June.

Macroeconomic data were generally favourable. Inflation was only 4.3%, compared with the 7.5% predicted. From January 2011, the Bank of Mozambique had cut the base rate – the rate at which the Bank lends to commercial banks, the 'Facilidade Permanente de Cedência' – 12 times, from 16.5% to 8.3% at the end of 2013. But the average rate for commercial bank loans remained a very high 20.3%. Mozambique's foreign debt reached $ 5.8 bn at the end of the year, which was 30% of GDP, according to Finance Minister Manuel Chang, and thus considered as sustainable. Most debt was long-term (20–50 years) with low interest rates. GDP growth was 7%. Agricultural production in the 2102/13 season was 2.2 m tonnes of cereals and 800,000 tonnes of tubers (cassava, sweet potato and potato).

The number of pupils per teacher in Mozambican *primary schools* had fallen considerably over the past four years – but classes remained overcrowded. Education Minister Augusto Jone said on 21 August that in in 2013 the ratio had fallen to 65 pupils to one teacher, from 76 to one in 2009.

LAM Mozambique Airlines Flight 470 crashed on 29 November into the Bwabwata National Park in Namibia en route from Maputo to Luanda (Angola), killing all 33 people on board. The *plane crash* was the airline's first fatal incident since 1970. Since 2011, all airlines certified in Mozambique had been banned from flying to Europe, and EU officials from flying in Mozambican planes, because of deficiencies, not in the airlines themselves, but in the regulatory agency, the Mozambican Civil Aviation Institute. *Wild animals* killed 59 people in the first five months of 2013; crocodiles continued to be the most deadly animals, killing 47. In addition, snakes killed six people, elephants three, and hippopotami three.

Printed in the United States
By Bookmasters